I Put A Spell On You

The Autobiography of

Nina Simone

with Stephen Cleary

I Put A Spell On You

Da Capo Press • New York

Library of Congress Cataloging in Publication Data

Simone, Nina, 1933–.
  I put a spell on you: the autobiography of Nina Simone / with Stephen
Cleary.—1st Da Capo Press ed.
      p.   c.
  Originally published: New York: Pantheon Books, c1991.
  Discography: p.
  Includes index.
  ISBN 0-306-80525-1
  1. Simone, Nina, 1933–   2. Singers—Biography. I. Cleary, Stephen. II.
Title.
[ML420.S5635A3 1993]
782.42164′092—dc20 —dc20 —dc20
[B]
[782.42164′092]   93-24645
[B]   CIP

First Da Capo Press edition 1993

This Da Capo Press paperback edition of *I Put A Spell on You*
is an unabridged republication of the edition published in
New York in 1992. It is reprinted by arrangement with
Pantheon Books, a division of Random House, Inc.

Published by Da Capo Press, Inc.
A Subsidiary of Plenum Publishing Corporation
233 Spring Street, New York, N.Y. 10013

Manufactured in the United States of America

To my mother, my daughter, and to the memory of my beloved father, John Divine Waymon.

Acknowledgements

It's nearly thirty years since I first started this book and through that time I received encouragement and support from many people. Friends like Mimi Saunders, Father Amdee, Dew Mason, Alice Johnson and family, Agnes Benjamin, Ina Langenburg, Frances Welsing, Claudette Johnson, Benis Farouk, Juliska van der Hoeven, Dr Patricia Holmes, Rock, Vital Gbezo, Imojah, Maxine Walters, Donald Shirley, my godmother Mrs Tubman, Mother Jerusalem, Professor Clemens Sandresky, Gerald Guess, Laurie Roland, Kim Novak, Lillian Lagarrique, Dr Beverley Robinson, Ivan Mogull, Nicolas Ashford, Valerie Simpson, Little Richard, Cicely Tyson, Sidney Poitier, Mark Penniman, Jewell and Bob Nemeroff, Eartha Kitt, Pete Townshend, John Lee Hooker, Patti Labelle, Richie Havens, Lena Horne, Diane Carroll, Bernard Purdey, Richard Pryor, Ron Dellums, 'Sabir', Payton Crossley, Lenny Hannibal, Babatundi Abdellah, Ed Brown, Mary Pat Kelly, Betty Carter, Tom Reid, Diane Amiel, Ted Axelrod, Betty Shabaz, Arthur Morrison, Mike Young, Alice Coltrane, Weldon Irvine Jnr, and Jean Adamo.

I owe a particular debt to all those people who kindly shared their memories of the times we shared together and who contributed more than they could know to the writing of this book: Andy Young, John Lewis, Miriam Makeba, Immam Jamil, Nikki Giovanni, Joanne McKnight, Susan Baumann, Josephine Jones, Stanley Wise and Michelle Kourouma. Special thanks also to the people who were at my side as I enjoyed or endured many of the events described in this book, to Al Schackman, Raymond Gonzalez, Gerrit de Bruin, Roland Grivelle, Leopoldo Fleming, Paul Robinson, Chris White, Jim Watkins, Roger Nupie, Olatunji, Stephen Ames-Brown, Willene Credle, Jackie Hammond, Anthony Sannucci, and Max Cohen.

It is impossible to thank some of the people who determined the direction of my life because they are no longer with us, but I salute the memory of Dr Martin Luther King Jnr, Malcolm X, Langston Hughes, President Seko Touré, Lorraine Hansberry, and James Baldwin. Among the living, I am proud to have walked alongside Amiri and Amina Baraka, Maya Angelou, Abbey Lincoln, Coretta Scott King, Dick Gregory, Angela Davis, James Forman, Odetta, Louis Farrakhan, Alex Haley and, most especially, Kwami Touré. Thanks and gratitude to Mayors James Sharpe, Maynard Jackson, Tom Bradley, and Marion Berry. Thanks also to Rowena Webb at Ebury Press.

Finally thanks and love to my family: my daughter Lisa, my mother, my brothers John Irvine, Carrol, Harold and Sam Waymon; my sisters Dorothy Simmons and Frances Fox; my nieces Crystal Fox, Anita Williams, Robin Thomas, and her husband John. Last of all I'd like to pay my respects to the memory of my uncle, Walter Waymon. I think he'd have been proud of me.

Nina Simone, Amsterdam, 1991.

Prologue

When I used to get blue years ago James Baldwin would say the same thing to me each time, 'This is the world you have made for yourself Nina, now you have to live in it.' Jimmy was always a man to see things as they really are and his gaze would never flinch no matter how unpleasant the things he saw were.

When you sit down to think about your life, as I have had to for this book, you have to look back over some things you've kept out of the daylight of your mind for years, and they can catch you. It might be a photograph of an old boyfriend found at the back of a drawer: you look at it and then feel a bundle of different reactions tumbling inside you, and you say to yourself, 'My God, I never knew he affected me so deeply!'

So I've spent a lot of time persuading those lost memories out of the shadows into the light. At times it wasn't easy, at others the dam broke in a rush and I was flooded by so many memories I lost count of them all. It's funny too how you don't have much control over what it is you do remember; how the most inconsequential, unimportant events sit in the front of your mind as clear as yesterday and the moments you just ache to relive stay out of reach for days or weeks at a time. Finally, when it's the last thing in the world you're thinking of, when you're staring out at the clouds through an airplane window or drinking tea and reading a magazine it all clicks on and those memories run through your head like a home movie, which just won't turn off when you want it to.

Luckily for me most of my clearest memories are also my happiest. Often you don't know how truly happy you were then until you look back and realize how much worse things could have been, how if certain things had turned out the slightest bit differently so many of your favourite people would never have crossed your path and what seemed at the time to be casual meetings and passing acquaintances would never have matured into deep, lifelong friendships.

I've criss-crossed the world many times and every big city holds its own treasure-box of memories. I've had lovers from many different countries and I've fallen in love with whole countries, and, in the case of Africa, with a whole continent. People say you should measure yourself by the friends you have, and when I look at mine I'm more than content to be me. Through my life I made a world for myself just as Jimmy said I would, and the best thing of all is that I'm still happy to live in it, after all these years.

Chapter 1

Around 1855 in North Carolina a shoot-out took place between some white settlers and the last band of hostile Indians left hiding out in the mountains. The settlers won, captured the Indian chief and hung him from the nearest tree. His name was Skyuka. The shoot-out was talked up over the years until it got to be known as the Battle of Round Mountain. With the Indians gone, the railroad company began laying a single track into the mountains, and four miles uphill of a little town called Landrum they built a passing station so a train going downhill could pull over and let an uphill one by. Next to the track they built a few houses to shelter the railroad workers during the winter. Then they started thinking about a name for this new town.

Someone suggested that they call it Skyuka after the lynched Indian chief, but the older folks didn't take to the idea of naming their town after a man they had once set swinging from a tree, so they called it Tryon City instead, after Tryon Peak which towered above them. In 1891 they dropped the city part and settled for plain Tryon, and that's how my home town was born.

Across the state line in South Carolina, in Chesney County, lived one Indian who managed to stay alive through those times. She was my great-great-grandmother, and she married an African slave. Chesney County was real plantation country, so that was only natural; the white man had probably killed most of her own people anyway. They had a child, a daughter, born into slavery. She too married a slave, and they in turn had a son, my grandfather – part Indian, part Negro. In old family photographs he is dark-skinned, but look at his face and you see Indian eyes staring back. Standing next to him is a small, light-skinned woman – my grandmother. She too had mixed blood: her mother was half-Irish, the result of a plantation relationship my family has never been too interested in exploring.

1

Their child, my mother, was born on 20 November 1902. She is still alive today and the blood in her veins is a rich mixture, drawn from white slave-owners, black slaves and the Indian people who were destroyed to make way for the plantations and the railroad.

Less is known about my father's family. His great-grandparents were slaves and his family came from Pendleton, South Carolina, a little way from Inman, where my mother was raised. Daddy was born in 1899. He met my mother in 1917 and they began courting as soon as he laid eyes on her. At least he told me so whenever I asked him how he and Momma got together. When they met, Daddy was an entertainer working around Pendleton. He had a white suit, wore spats and danced; sang a little too, and played harmonica. Momma used to play piano for him while he danced and sang – something she never talked about to us children because by the time we were grown enough to be interested in hearing about her courting days Momma had become a church minister, and had put sinful things behind her: Daddy hadn't been singing hymns and spirituals in that white suit.

Exactly what the fifteen ministers in my mother's immediate family thought about Daddy's life as an entertainer never got passed on, but they approved of his name because he was christened John Divine Waymon, after St John the Divine, the author of the Book of Revelation. My mother was christened Mary Kate – Mary after Jesus's mother, Kate perhaps as a memento of her Irish great-grandfather. I never had the nerve to ask her about that.

They were married in Inman in 1922. The next year my brother John Irvine was born, and the year after that my sister Lucille. Dad kept Mom busy and the next year she gave birth to twins, my brothers Carrol and Harold. At just six weeks old Harold caught spinal meningitis. In those days there wasn't much that could be done about a disease like that, and it was assumed Harold would die. He didn't, but he was very young for such a hard fight and the disease left him paralysed down one side. When Harold was grown, the family would hold up his first few weeks as evidence of his fighting spirit. Harold was tough all right – so tough you could almost call him mean. Maybe that was because he never forgave the world for the injustice it had inflicted on him.

Apart from Harold's struggle, these were good times for my parents. Mom stayed at home raising the children and Daddy worked in a dry-cleaning plant. I mean worked. He was a clever man; although he wasn't educated he had a genius for getting on. Whatever job he was doing, he took the time to learn all about it; when he knew the details of his job he'd set about watching the people working around him and pretty soon he'd know their jobs too. And just as important, he knew how to get himself liked and respected. It didn't mean a thing to him whether he worked for a white boss or a black boss, and he was respected equally by both. He turned his hand to anything: he was a trained barber, he knew the dry-cleaning business inside out and while he was doing one or other of those jobs he worked in a truck haulage business on the side.

By the end of the twenties my family was doing all right. Daddy might have been content to sit back and reflect how far he had come in less than ten years, but that wasn't his way; his ambition was to do much more than just get by. He didn't want to work for any boss – white, black, blue or green. He wanted to make it on his own, and the more he thought about it the more he realized it wasn't going to happen in Inman, South Carolina. He was looking around for new opportunities when my mother got pregnant again. That didn't stop him in what he decided to do.

While he was driving trucks Daddy had taken a load some thirty miles up to a small town in the North Carolina mountains. He made a friend there, a black man like him who talked about setting up on his own with a road haulage business. They talked about the idea every time Daddy was passing through, but the problem was money: with a family to feed and another baby on the way he couldn't put his hands on what was needed to get the business going. It seemed like just another dream to dream while he drove trucks through the night, until he stopped off to see his friend one more time and was told that the small town was looking for a new barber.

It was the solution to the problem. Daddy could work as a barber and help run the trucks the rest of the time. Any extra money from the barber shop could go into the haulage side. It didn't take long to figure out. So Daddy took on the barber shop and the family moved to North Carolina. Momma was eight months pregnant and hadn't been in her new home more than a couple of weeks before she gave birth to my sister Dorothy on 7 March 1929.

The small town was Tryon. By the time my family moved there it had come quite a way from just a few huts slung up around the railtrack. Over the years it had become popular as a resort. Tryon lay in the shadow of what the locals called Hogback Mountain, which sheltered it from the worst of the weather so it was cool during summer and pleasant in winter. Summer in the south can get hotter than hell, and white folks came from as far away as Florida to escape the heat and try out Tryon's main attractions – horses and moonshine whisky.

My parents were very happy. Daddy was working for himself at last and Mom had a big new house to settle into. The children were busy exploring a strange new world of forests and horses. But there was more to it than that – there was the special nature of Tryon itself. It was the south and it was 1929, but as a resort town Tryon had developed in an uncommon way. For instance there wasn't a black side of town: it was more like a series of circles around the centre with blacks or whites living in these circles. And a few blacks, a few, lived almost in the centre, almost in the white areas. It was a checkerboard type of living, with areas that were totally white and a few pockets of blacks.

The place existed mainly by taking care of the needs of visitors, so in their everyday lives black and white townspeople mixed together all the time. Tryon was laid out in a kind of L-shape, with one of the legs being the main street. That's where my father had his barber shop and dry-cleaning business. Most of the customers for dry cleaning were white, but nearly all of the customers for haircuts were black. There was another barber shop a little way up the main street where the white folks got their haircuts. The man who owned that place was also black, although he could have passed for white and was regarded as a white man so long as he had a pair of scissors in his hand. He lived a little way up the street from my parents – a black man outside of working hours.

However, in the schools, hotels, restrooms – all the places people come into intimate contact – Tryon was like any other southern town at that time – segregated. All the same, because the town was physically more mixed than usual, blacks and whites took part in all sorts of activities together long before desegregation. People played football constantly, teams from the white schools playing against teams from the black schools. The same for baseball. Black and white church ministers met on an individual basis nearly every day. Each year there would be special church services: one Sunday the congregation of a black church would go to a white church to worship,

4

the next week the white congregation would go to the black church.

Relations between the black and white community were always very cordial: of course there was no policy of racial justice in Tryon, it was just an easygoing small town with a council which existed only to ensure nothing happened to spoil the peaceful life the white folks led.

Daddy's barber shop was usually busy and the dry cleaning really took off. But he hadn't forgotten the plans for the trucking business: he got it going with his partner as soon as he could, and he was right about it being the smartest thing he could do. After about a year they bought their own truck, driving loads through the night and at weekends.

My family lived in a big house then – it had a slide in the yard, a swing and a basketball hoop, and we were one of only two black families in town with a tennis court next to the house, so other kids were always around going to and fro. By 1930 my father was a respected member of the town's business community, Momma had made a good home and my brothers and sisters had settled in school and were doing well.

Social life mainly revolved around church. The biggest churches in town were the Methodists and the Baptists, followed by the Episcopalians. At the bottom was the Holiness church, the Holy-rollers, who were looked down on by the others. It was a social thing, because the Holiness congregation came mostly from the poorest part of town. Of all the churches the Holiness was the most integrated, because at the lowest level Tryon was racially mixed anyhow. Down the street from where we lived there was a family with a white mother and black children. Nobody remarked on it – that was how it was for the poorest of the poor.

My family were Methodists. Daddy was a church deacon and Momma an elder, one of the 'Saints', who dressed all in white to worship and helped the minister run the church along with the deacons. Life at home was run along very strict rules: there was never liquor in the house and there was no profanity. A Christian household.

But then the Depression came. Tryon was a resort town and the first things to go when money gets short are luxuries like a trip to the mountains. The summer trade started to dry up, and by the winter of 1931 the place was like a ghost town. More than half of the dry cleaning Daddy handled in his shop came from visitors to the town, and that business just vanished. Even though my father and his partner laid off the drivers they had, haulage work became more and more scarce and they weren't making the money to meet the payments on the truck. Any money that the barber shop made went on feeding the family. There was a little saved, but that soon got spent. One morning my brothers looked out of the window at the front of the house and the truck was gone. Momma had always taken really good care of the garden, growing vegetables, canning fruit and keeping a few chickens. It was lucky she did, because that winter the garden kept them from starving. By Christmas 1931 the barber shop, dry cleaners and truck were gone. Daddy was busted.

Momma had never worked outside the home but she had to now. Daddy took any type of work that he could get, but most of the time he couldn't get any type of work at all. My mother took a job cleaning the windows in the town centre on Saturday mornings and Carrol, who was then aged six, once went along to help her. He stuck at it all morning then walked home beside her carrying the bucket. When they got back to the house Carrol ran round the back to hide so no one would see him crying at the shame of seeing his mother working like that, in full view of anybody who passed by. Momma never asked him to help clean windows again. When things got really bad the government set up a relief centre where women could go to sew army uniforms for a couple of dollars a week. That work was what they would usually give to the guys in the penitentiary, but it was how my family survived 1932.

The next year Daddy got a break. The Federal Government was providing food to the poor through the National Relief Agency and they located the delivery trucks for our area in Tryon. They needed local drivers, and my father was offered a job. There were two benefits: first, there was a regular wage again – although it was tiny, it was regular; second, Daddy was taking food from the depot and delivering it all around. Not only did the men at the depot get given a little extra food to take home, but the drivers built up a network of people who would trade food among themselves. Our garden was my parents' pride now and Daddy would take whatever we had left over, like collard greens, string beans, tomatoes and sometimes eggs, to swap with people who had more sugar or flour, say, than they needed. He was still wheeling and dealing like always, even though the road ahead must have seemed dark as Christmas 1932 approached. It was a time for tightening belts, scratching a living and praying for a change in the right direction. A change was on its way all right, although it probably wasn't exactly what Daddy had in mind. Momma neither. At the end of the summer that year she got pregnant again. She was going to have another baby. Me.

I was born at home at six in the morning. On my birth certificate Daddy listed his occupation as 'barber', although he hadn't been that for almost two years. Momma was down as 'housewife', although she had been working right up to the week I was delivered. They still had their pride. I was christened Eunice Kathleen Waymon. Six months after I was born Daddy went off the NRA programme because at last they had started to open up some of the hotels again. A lakeside camp had opened for business and they took Daddy on as a cook, so again we had a steady supply of food in our kitchen. Daddy thought he was out of the woods and it would only be a question of time before our family would be up and moving. In the meantime, one way or another he was making enough to feed all his family, including the new baby.

Most of what I remember from the very earliest part of my life is tied up with food and music. My first memory is of my mother's singing. When she was around the house she sang all the time, in a high, trilling voice. She sang the same songs she'd sing at Bible meetings and they became the soundtrack to my infant life: 'I'll Fly Away' and 'If You Pray Right' or 'Heaven Belongs to Me'. While she baked she would sit me up on the counter-top and give me an empty jam-jar to cut out the biscuit shapes in the dough, singing all the while. It seemed to me that she performed miracles every day. When the other children had gone out she'd look down at me and say, 'Eunice, I don't know where I'm going to get dinner.' We'd look around to see what there was in the kitchen and she'd be right, there was nothing there. Dinnertime would come around and out would come what she called the Waymon Specials. Vinegar pie, made with apple cider vinegar and dough. Dumplings, chicken or – if the twins had picked any – blackberry. A lot of dumplings, always set down on the table with the same announcement, 'This stretches the meal'. Rice pudding, brown betty. And beans. Tons of beans. When all those beans got on top of us Momma would put sugar on them and create a whole new delicacy. We were poor for a long time but I can't remember ever going hungry, not once. Momma made sure of that.

7

The small garden that kept us alive during the worst of the Depression soon became a big garden, then a huge garden and finally a little farm. We had hogs, chickens and a cow. Rows and rows of string beans, collard greens, tomatoes, corn and squash. The only things I liked that we didn't grow were bananas, but when Daddy realized how much I liked them he took to bringing one home with him every night. As soon as I heard his car coming I'd jump off the porch, run to the gap in the fence and wait for him to drive past. He'd slow down, I'd jump up on to the running board, reach through the open window for my banana and be halfway through finishing it before he even turned into the driveway. Sometimes he'd pass by the house altogether and we'd go up around the block with me on the running board pulling faces at him, going bug-eyed trying to make him laugh so that he'd have to stop whistling. He'd set his face serious like he was in church and look over his nose at me, whistling all the while. He could keep that whistling going a long time, but I always made him laugh in the end.

When I was three I saw snow for the first time, or at least that's the first time I remember it. I didn't know what it was; it frightened me seeing the garden so changed and I could see that the animals didn't like it. All in all, winter seemed like a mean trick to play for four months of the year. My eldest sister, Lucille, talked about new games like sledging and snowmen but every time I got ready to go out with my brothers and sisters Momma would call me to her. She was worried about me catching cold, so I spent winter in the kitchen. I didn't really mind too much – it was where the stove was and it was warm and Momma would be cooking or washing and singing along. Snowmen could wait for a year.

Hog-killing time was different – that was real fun. The doomed animal was well fed through summer and most of the fall, and then just before winter began Daddy would crack the hog's skull with his axe and it would shuffle down on to its knees and die. Then the hard work started. While Momma and my sisters were getting everything ready in the kitchen my father and brothers would be burning the carcass, getting rid of the hair and lifting the hog into a huge black pot to boil over a fire. Then Daddy would skin the hog, hang the body up on the back porch and its insides would be cut out, ready to be canned and cooked for the winter. Some of the meat would be salted, some smoked, the rest roasted. For the next few days the kitchen was filled with sausages, sweetbreads and hanging roasts and there was pork crackling with every meal. Standing in that kitchen with the smell of roasting pork so strong I could almost reach out and touch it, I knew what people meant when they talked about hog heaven. I knew what it was to be happy.

I was at the age where every day brought a new experience and in my innocence I enjoyed every moment without stopping to think about what it meant. It was a time made all the more special because my childhood was forced to end within a year of that first remembered winter. Everything was so simple – all I had to do was stay close to Momma, and looking at her then, from across the years, and at myself, I miss the certainty of a time when if she'd have told me to put my hand into the fire I would have done it without question, knowing she was right. I cannot remember a single occasion when she raised her voice to me. All she had to say was 'Eunice, you did something wrong,' and I would go down to the basement and cry myself half to death. Struggling out of the Depression must have been so hard for my mother and father, especially since they had known what it was like to be doing well, but I never knew anything of their troubles; at home we were happy. We must have been, because although I might not have completely understood what was going on I was an intuitive child – I would have sensed something and I would have been unhappy too. And I never was, until Daddy almost died and the innocent days had to come to a close.

In 1935 we moved house. My father had stopped working at the lake camp and spent most of his time in the garden. The new house was smaller and the bedrooms were upstairs and at the back so at night you had to go out of the house and up the outside staircase to bed. We moved because we didn't have the money to stay in the big house. There was still very little work around for my father, so Momma took a job housekeeping for a white family in Tryon. Nobody knew that Daddy was sick and the main reason he decided to stay at home was he didn't know if he could hold down a regular job. We had been in the new house less than a year before the stove caught fire in the middle of the night and it burnt down. We all ran down those outside stairs into the yard and watched while it burned and the men dashed in and out of the fire saving what they could.

We moved again, to a house above an Episcopal School Centre. This was meant as a temporary measure while we found somewhere decent. Then suddenly finding a new house was forgotten. Daddy was taken ill in the middle of the night and driven to hospital. He had a blockage in his intestine and the local doctor couldn't deal with it.

When Daddy got to the hospital it was decided he would need an operation, one of the first of its type in the world. They had to take his stomach out and wash it, and once that was done he was left with a huge wound which would have to heal of its own accord in the open air, exposed to the sun. Weeks passed with Momma going back and forth to the hospital not knowing if Daddy would ever come home.

Slowly he got his strength back – at least enough strength to leave hospital – and we got the house ready for him. I thanked God he had made it. I knew that Momma would have to work and my brothers and sisters would be at school all day so I would be my father's nurse. We talked about it and Momma knew she could trust me. There would be no more sitting around the house listening to Momma's singing, no more dancing around the garden pretending to help Daddy milk the cow. I was almost four years old and my carefree childhood was over.

Daddy came home just as summer started, and was laid out on a cot in the sun. He had always been thin, so thin that his trousers slipped down his behind, but now he was skinnier than a twig. He couldn't hardly walk at all and at first he didn't speak much, either, but just lay in the sun, resting. The wound from his operation was a great ugly thing with a tube coming out of it which drained fluid from his stomach. The doctors had done all they could, and now it was a question of Daddy healing himself. So he lay outside and I kept washing him, more than ten times a day, trying to keep that wound clean. He couldn't take solid food, so the two of us would spend the morning working out what mix of liquid ingredients would go together for lunch each day. His favourite was a mixture of raw eggs beaten up with a little sugar and vanilla, mixed with Carnation milk. I liked it, too, although I only took a tiny sip each time because I knew we had to make him better. Years later the memory of that Carnation milk would begin one of the strangest episodes of my life and bind me to my father for ever, but back then I was just happy he could keep it down. Slowly, Daddy improved. After a couple of months he was able to take a few steps, then he got himself a cane and with me on one side and the cane on the other we would walk round the garden. Once we had that licked we started going up the road a little, Daddy stopping to talk along the way. Everyone always wanted to know how he was, even though they might have had the same conversation the day before. 'J.D.' was what everybody called him, his initials. 'Hey, J.D.!' they would shout from across the street, and Daddy would lean down on my shoulder while he raised the cane in his other hand to wave. He would have to stop to talk every few yards, and if people didn't notice that Daddy was getting tired I'd pull on his arm a couple of times until he started to move away.

As his crisis passed, our other problems came crowding back in. The Episcopal Centre where we lived was cramped and uncomfortable: people were around the school during the day, and Daddy didn't have the peace and quiet he needed. We had to move, that was definite. The problem was how to pay for it now Daddy wasn't working, and it was certain he wasn't going to be able to for a long time. We were poorer than we had been during the worst of the Depression and the only place we could afford to move to was a tiny house in Lynn, a small settlement about thirteen miles east of Tryon.

Lynn was primitive – really primitive. It was set back in the woods, a collection of falling-down houses barely clinging on to the hillside. Several black families lived there already but when we arrived we were the first family to build an outside bathroom. Up to that time everyone else had just gone off into the woods. I remember Carrol laughing at the notion that the Waymons had brought the outhouse to Lynn, like some kind of pioneer missionaries. It was just as well that we could laugh about things like that, otherwise we would have broken down and cried.

Even so, if you turned your back on the houses and looked into the woods you realized that Lynn was set in one of the most beautiful forests you would see anywhere. The move gave Daddy what he needed: peace, quiet, fresh air, and time. While Momma went to work in Tryon and the other children were at school, Daddy and I set about the garden. At first he directed me from his chair; then, as he got stronger, he moved up and down the rows himself, planting seeds, pruning back, pointing out the weeds for me to collect. When we got tired we'd sit back down and play patty-cake or just talk.

It was accepted by all my brothers and sisters that I was Daddy's favourite; he'd come right out and say so if anybody asked. There were special things the two of us did together, things that no one else was interested in. He loved his car, but everyone apart from me

11

thought it was the funniest thing they had ever seen. John Irvine wouldn't even sit in it to go to church; he said he'd rather walk. Momma sat in it but pretended it was a Rolls-Royce, ignoring the snorts and explosions as it chugged down the road. But Daddy and I loved it. We washed it whenever the mood came over us, snuck out for drives together when nobody was watching, and when Daddy was too sick to drive but well enough to walk a little we'd sit in the car just to enjoy the feel of it. The day Daddy knew he was better was the day he started driving again.

We came out of his sickness buddies, inseparable. There are no words to describe how happy we were together. By force of circumstance Momma wasn't around like she had been, so I slipped out from under her apron straight into my father's arms, and to be truthful I never missed her for more than a passing moment. Daddy was always fun. He had a way of gently kidding my mother that would make me put my hand in my mouth to stop laughing out loud. He was always a well-dressed man, but when he and Momma had to be especially smart he would come into the kitchen wearing a good suit, beautiful shirt, beautiful tie, as neat as a pin except for the great muddy galoshes untied around his feet. He usually appeared like this on a Sunday-go-to-meeting day and wouldn't say a thing about his boots until Momma noticed. Momma always noticed. Daddy would stand there quietly, mischief in his eyes, while she told him off. And I'd be behind Momma with my hand stuffed halfway down my throat, not daring to look him in the face.

Except for one time when I was much older, he always told me the truth. Whatever I asked him he answered honestly as best he could; he never ducked an awkward question and he never lied. I asked whatever questions came into my head. Sometimes I threw him a real curve ball. When I was about six and a half I got to be obsessed with the idea of our family improving itself, and it caused me all kinds of problems because of my brother Harold. Although he tried to be independent, Harold needed a lot of attention on account of his paralysis, and it seemed to me that without meaning to he was holding us back. This was tied in with my fear of some neighbours of ours at the time, the Knoxes. Back then I didn't know what rickets was; I just knew that the Knox family were cripples, nearly all of them, and the way they looked frightened me. There was another crippled woman living directly across the street. It felt like these people were all around us. They scared me and I began to think that they were holding the rest of us back, that they were the problem.

I kept these ideas to myself for a while until one afternoon I said to my father – and I can remember exactly how I said it – I said, 'You have to get rid of Harold because we're a black family and he's gonna hold us down and we have to move fast.' Daddy didn't raise an eyebrow. He asked me what I meant and I struggled to explain. He understood the mess of thoughts I was having and waited until I finished. Then he put me straight. He said that what had happened to Harold and to the Knoxes was not their fault; they were trying to live with dignity and pride like everyone else, and it was harder for them. If I was fortunate enough to be physically strong then I should help anyone less fortunate, not leave them behind. And if we were going to get anywhere as a family then it would be with Harold or not at all, because what kind of family would we be if we just forgot about him when things were tough? I didn't say anything. Then he asked if I would feel the same way if I'd been the one that caught meningitis instead of Harold. I had to answer no.

Daddy left it at that. He knew all sorts of ideas were running through my mind and I had to learn to make sense of them myself, so he just pointed me in the right direction. That was how Daddy was; always around to help, but allowing me space to grow. For the rest of my childhood I relied on him more than anyone else in the world, and he never let me down. Never. If other things started to get too much, I knew I could run to him. He became my refuge: from church, from Momma and from music.

Chapter 2

Everything that happened to me as a child involved music. It was part of everyday life, as automatic as breathing. As well as piano Daddy played guitar and harmonica and led the choir in church; Momma played piano and sang too. My brothers and sisters all played piano and sang in the church choir, smaller gospel groups, glee clubs and at other social events. Everybody played music. There was never any formal training; we learned to play the same way we learned to walk, it was that natural. At the time I was born we didn't have a piano in the house, we had a pedal organ. When our house was burned down, the pedal organ was the first thing rescued out of the fire.

As a baby I always reacted to the sound of music. I would raise myself up on my arms and look around whenever music started playing, and if I was crying I would stop the moment it started. When I was still in my crib I was taken to church, and the ladies there looked down at me and saw that I was clapping along to the hymns. Not just waving my hands, but clapping in time to the music. That was the important thing, the fact that I was clapping in time, and all sorts of remarks were made about how I was obviously blessed.

Music was played at home any time of the day or night. My brothers and sisters would fight to get to the organ first and then wrestle to keep possession of the stool. Music stopped for dinner, but often John Irvine would eat sitting on the organ lid so he'd get to play it first when the meal was over.

So when I was very young it was assumed I would have musical talent even if I didn't yet have the strength to push down the keys on the organ. Eventually I grew enough to be able to climb up on to the stool and sit at the keyboard. This was when I was two and a half. No one noticed until a couple of months later when Momma came into the living room and heard me playing one of her favourite hymns,

'God Be with You 'Til We Meet Again', in the key of F. She was so surprised she almost died on the spot. No one had heard me trying to play the organ before – not even messing around trying out the sound of the notes. The whole family was astonished. Baby Eunice, whom they had never even seen sit at the organ before, was now playing hymns straight through without a mistake. Daddy just smiled and shook his head. To Momma's mind there was only one explanation: I had received a gift from God.

In the outside world we already had a reputation as an exceptional family. Daddy had become a pillar of the black community – if he did hit hard times during the Depression then so had everyone else, and at least he'd been able to keep his family clothed and fed. My mother was equally well regarded. When she first came to Tryon her baking and picnics established her in the circle of respected ladies and made her a favourite of their children. She became an elder of the Methodist congregation and within months was one of its most important members; by the time I was three years old she had become an ordained Methodist minister and was preaching in churches all around the area. She did all this while bringing up six children, working to support her family and nursing her husband through a long and nearly fatal illness.

These achievements were impressive enough, but my parents gained real respect for the way they were as people. They could have been arrogant or boastful about themselves or their family, but they weren't – they just got on with things and tried to live a decent Christian life.

We Waymon children had the same reputation with the other kids in town. John Irvine was one of the best sportsmen Tryon ever had: he excelled at any game he played, especially baseball, everybody's favourite. Lucille was smart as a whip at school, liked and respected in church, a godsend to her mother and pretty with it. Carrol was an academic star winning all the school prizes, a leading light in the choir – like his father – and one of the funniest kids in town. Harold, with all his disadvantages, also shone in school and most of the time carried himself with dignity and fortitude. Dorothy was like Lucille, only prettier. This was the family I was born into. By the outside world I was expected to excel.

And we were all preacher's children, which meant we had a responsibility for the position of our family in the church and the

15

community. We were expected to be the best in everything we did, yet at the same time behave with modesty and humility.

When we walked off the street and through the front door of our house a different set of rules applied. Out in the world the Waymon children might be shining examples to kids everywhere, but at home you sat down and ate humble pie with every meal. The view was, any talent you had was given by God so there was no reason for you to be proud of it – you were just fortunate. And if you worked hard to develop your talent that wasn't anything to be proud of either; it was sinful not to nurture any gift you had. You should be grateful to God for the gift, and non-competitive – that was important.

The philosophy in our family was that you didn't outshine anyone; you developed the talent you had, but it was there to be shared with everyone else, not hoarded away. So when I came along playing entire hymns by ear the first lesson I learned was not to be big-headed about it, and I wasn't. As soon as the townspeople got to hear me play they started to call me a 'prodigy', but I didn't know what words like that meant and no one at home thought it important enough to explain.

As far as church was concerned Momma was a fanatic. She wasn't unusual – plenty of southern Evangelical families were like ours, quite a few of them in Tryon. But Momma took her religion a stage further and became a minister, which meant she had to travel all around preaching and leading services. By the time I was four the church had come to dominate her life. At home we had always been a devout family, so as far as the way we lived was concerned not much changed. But as I grew older I came to realize something about my mother which was difficult to accept: her first loyalty was to God and her ministry. It came before anything else – before her husband, before her family and before me.

Momma had a name for any sort of music that wasn't religious, that was 'of the world'. She called it 'real' music. If I played a tune I'd heard somewhere she'd say: 'Don't play any of those real songs.' For a long time I thought that 'real' was the name for a style of music, like 'blues' or 'gospel'. Very soon after I started playing Momma took me preaching with her, to open the service. I was just over three and a half years old and my legs were too short for my feet to reach the piano pedals, but I'd play the opening hymn at the service, sort of introducing Momma. She knew what a sensation her tiny girl caused with congregations that had never seen me play before, and it was a good way of catching people's attention before she started preaching. I got to know the inside of a good many churches and fell asleep on the back seats of dozens of cars as they drove Momma and me home at night.

By the time I was six I was the regular pianist at our church in Tryon. In those days music involved no effort; the piano was a wonderful toy that I could play for hours without getting tired and although Momma tried to push my music down one particular road I had no preference for any individual style. In fact I liked to play as many different styles as possible, though I had to keep an eye out for Momma if I started wandering off the heavenly track. Luckily I had an extra pair of eyes to help me, because not everyone in my family was as hostile to 'real songs' as she was.

Daddy wasn't. He knew a whole load of songs from his bachelor days and he would sing them to me and I'd try to play by ear, or he'd play it himself. I never noticed for years that when Daddy played piano he only used the black keys: Irving Berlin played the same way, so there can't be much wrong with it. I must have been listening so hard for the tune that I never watched what his hands were doing. Daddy's favourite was 'The Darktown Strutters' Ball' and he'd sneak up in the day when Momma was out and get me to play it. He'd sit by the window or outside on the porch, and if he saw Momma coming down the road he'd whistle – the signal for me to switch to a more righteous tune.

That's not to say I didn't like holy music: I loved it. Church taught me rhythm, and it's been a vital part of my music ever since. I liked the music in the Holiness church most of all. Their prayer meetings were one great commotion, with people testifying and shouting all night. The music that went along with it had incredible rhythm, it sounded like it came straight out of Africa, and I took to going to the Holiness services every week just to get into that beat. Their services were always lively, but when revival time came round they just went crazy. The Holiness church was on the lower road, a little way from our Methodist chapel and when we'd be having our own service you could hear their revival drums beating and the testifying going on above the sound of our singing.

Our church was quite small – it fitted in about two hundred people and got pretty warm in summer. No air conditioning of course – just fans flapping away. I'd go to church at nine in the morning on

17

Sundays for the first service, play for the Sunday school at eleven, play for the choir, play for the programmes at three and finish off playing at the six o'clock service. I had an hour's break between four and five. Then I played on Wednesday night at the prayer meeting and Friday night at choir practice. And went to the Holiness church too. I did this every week between the ages of four and twelve until I left Tryon to go to high school, so it was lucky for me that I liked playing in church – though after a while the routine started to get boring, especially once I started taking piano lessons and learning about all sorts of music I had never come across before.

That was during normal services. It was entirely different at revival time, when you rededicated yourself to God and the congregation would get hold of sinners who had stopped coming to church and get them to repent. You'd get rebaptised too, sometimes. I remember when I was twelve Momma saying to us children, 'I'm giving you back to God!', and we were baptised again, in a pool, totally immersed. Or she'd say we'd backslid, and had to recommit ourselves to the Lord. At revivals, out-of-town preachers would come in, go to a different person's house each night, eat fried chicken, then preach. There would be a prayer meeting every night for two weeks, starting at seven in the evening and finishing around eleven.

The church would be packed full with the church ladies, the Saints, looking crisp and clean in their white dresses, stockings and shoes, fanning a mile a minute. The preacher would be going, he'd be preaching, he'd be carrying on and everybody'd be going 'Amen!' and 'Yes Lord!' Then someone would start to testify, shouting and tearing up, speaking in tongues, with those fans going crazy all around and people running up and down the aisle – just running back and forth with other people shouting, praising the Lord and the preacher gathering up all that spiritual energy and throwing it back out on the people. Women would have to go to hospital sometimes, they got so transported.

While this was going on I'd be playing the piano, gospel music. The repeated rhythm was part of the process. Someone would start off a song and I'd pick it up and keep playing. The person that had started it off might start to come through themselves so my job was to keep that rhythm repeating, building on it, keeping the feeling going. Sometimes it was hard not to leap away from the keyboard and run down the aisle myself.

When the meetings were over I would walk home in a dream, drunk with it all, heady with the shouting and dancing and singing. I'd get home, sleep like a log, and when I woke in the morning the first thing I'd think about was doing it all over again that night.

Gospel music was mostly improvisation within a fixed framework and it never occurred to me to analyse it. Gospel was part of church, which was part of normal life, and you don't sit around wondering exactly how it is you walk, or breathe, or do any other everyday thing. Even so, gospel taught me about improvisation, how to shape music in response to an audience and then how to shape the mood of the audience in response to my music. When I played I could take a congregation where I wanted – calm them down or lift them up until they became completely lost in the music and atmosphere. Of course God, the church and His ministers provided the spiritual inspiration, but the music was part of it too. At that time I learned valuable lessons in musical technique that had nothing to do with all the classical training that was to come. Over the years those lessons slipped into my blood and became part of me. A time would come when I would start to look for my own musical voice, and the lessons I learned from gospel music would help me find it.

Although Momma was now a Methodist minister her work in church didn't pay well. It wasn't supposed to; money raised in church collections paid for the transportation of the visiting preacher, and what was left went to the poor, or to the church itself. Daddy was still too weak to take a regular job so Momma worked as a housekeeper for a white family, Mr and Mrs Miller. Daddy would work occasionally, most often in the open air as a handyman or a gardener, but for the next few years the regular money came from Momma. By now my eldest brother John Irvine was a young man and he started working too, as well as Lucille, my eldest sister. So more money was coming in.

At last, in 1938, we had enough money to move back into Tryon, leaving the beautiful woods and primitive sanitation of Lynn behind us forever.

By now I was starting to get excited at the idea of starting school. Carrol and Harold were always talking about it, and I knew it was almost as important as church to my parents. No matter how small the house we lived in, there was always room to spread out books and get on with homework. Tryon had its own black junior school

19

with about 150 pupils, five teachers and a principal. The teachers were always ladies; for my first two years I had Mrs Hannon, after that Mrs McKissick. The principal was a man, but I don't recall his name. You only saw him at assembly or, if you misbehaved, in his office with a switch in his hand. That never happened to me – I was a preacher's child.

In school the kids were mixed together. If you didn't pass the exam at the end of the year you stayed down in your grade. Some kids never passed, so you ended up with some pretty large classmates. I found schoolwork easy, liked doing the examinations and always came out of them with straight As. If there was anything I found difficult I could always ask my brothers, who had done the same stuff a few years before.

Momma's becoming a minister meant certain changes at home. She was already working as a housekeeper so Momma had to fit in all her new work as a minister on top of that. She was a good preacher, in demand for revivals all over Polk County and down in South Carolina, so she did a lot of travelling. And there were the church conventions, when all the ministers would gather together for conferences. All in all, a lot of time away from home. Daddy was around, but work around the house fell on to Lucille's shoulders.

Lucille took on the burden of the house without complaint. Pretty soon she had us all running the way she wanted; she'd make the fire in the morning, cook our breakfast, walk us to school, make lunch and dinner and clean up the house. There was no nonsense with Lucille. She was a woman on fire, burning with energy. And tough when she had to be. Carrol and Harold were fighting one time when Harold got so mad he picked up a poker to hit Carrol. Lucille floored him like a prizefighter and when she saw Carrol sniggering she laid him out, too. But at the same time when I started to take an interest in feminine things it was she who guided me along the way. Lucille would bath me, plait my hair and talk about boys and what she thought of them, which wasn't much.

She had many admirers, but when they fell for her someone should have taken them aside and given them a friendly warning. The older ones would come round and sit talking with my father with the idea that they could impress her by getting friendly with Daddy, talking man-to-man. He never told them that there was no guaranteed way to get Lucille madder. And she dealt with these boyfriends the same way she did with us, tolerating no nonsense. We felt sorry for them.

Lucille was pretty, knew all about make-up, had a fine taste in clothes and loved to wear high-heeled shoes. She explained about perfume and fine lingerie, and taught me that a single top-quality dress was better than four or five cheap ones and it was always worth sacrificing quantity for quality. By the time I was ten years old Lucille understood my moods even better than Daddy, although he never stopped trying. She knew I loved her, and that if I treated her cruelly sometimes it was because I wanted it to be my mother who taught me these women's things, not her. And if Lucille resented that she was made a substitute Momma while all her girlfriends were getting married she never showed it, and until she left home no one knew her as well as me. I cried for days when she got married. I couldn't have had a more sensitive sister and she helped me get through what hurt most: I missed Momma all the time.

What little time I did get with Momma was often spent at the house of Mrs Miller, her employer. On Saturday mornings I would walk over to Mrs Miller's house and sit in the kitchen waiting for Momma to finish so we could walk home together. This was when I was five and a half. Mrs Miller was about the first white person I knew at all, to speak to. I liked her – she was always very kind and she had shocking white hair, which I loved. She had a boy named David living with her, although I don't think he was her son. I liked him too; we would play together while I was waiting for Momma to finish up. Sometimes Mrs Miller would drive Momma and me home in her car and often David would come along then stay at our house to play with me and my brothers. Mrs Miller would drive by later to pick him up.

Mrs Miller knew me quite well: she'd heard Momma talk about me, and one day when I was playing for a choir in town she decided to come and hear me for herself. She heard me play and told my mother that with the talent I had it would be sinful if I didn't have proper piano tuition.

Momma told her the truth – that we couldn't afford piano lessons. Mrs Miller thought about it for a couple of seconds and then came up with the answer: she would pay for me to have lessons for a year, and when it was over, if I showed promise, then a way would be found to ensure they continued. Momma was grateful and thanked God for the blessing. Daddy was grateful and thanked Mrs Miller. Lucille was grateful and started looking around for a piano tutor before Mrs Miller changed her mind. She didn't have to: Mrs Miller knew exactly who my tutor would be – an Englishwoman who had moved to Tryon with her Russian husband, a painter.

Her name was Mrs Muriel Massinovitch. In a couple of days it was all arranged: I would walk to the house in the woods on Saturday morning, have my piano lesson and then stop by Mrs Miller's to meet Momma and go home with her. It was about a two-mile walk. I crossed the railroad track, stopped at Owen's Pharmacy for a grilled cheese sandwich, ate it outside because they wouldn't let a black girl sit down in the drugstore, then went for my lesson. I followed that routine every Saturday morning for the next five years.

The first time I went to Mrs Massinovitch's house I almost fainted – it was so beautiful. The ground floor was one great open space with a big north-facing skylight in the roof. Mr Massinovitch used the light which flooded into the room to paint by and his easels were set up at one end of the room, surrounded by paints and sketchbooks. At the other end were two pianos, an upright and a concert grand. Halfway up the wall above the pianos a gallery jutted out into the room, and that was where they had their bedroom. If Mr Massinovitch wanted to paint the mountains towards Asheville all he had to do was walk up a few stairs to the gallery, set up his easel and look out through the skylight. The kitchen was down in the basement. The main room was full of flowers and their scent mixed with and softened that of the paint. With the sunlight coming through the roof and the smell of flowers and paint in the air, walking into that room was like walking into a sweet haze. I had never seen anything like it. When the front door shut behind me Tryon seemed so far away it could have been on another planet for all I knew or cared.

That first Saturday morning when I walked in my new tutor was standing by the grand piano. I thought then the same thing I thought every time I saw her for the next forty-five years: how could one person be so elegant? The first time I met Mrs Massinovitch she must have been about fifty-five years old, but she looked anything between thirty and eighty. She was petite, like a little bird. Her hair was silvery and tied up in a bun and when she opened her mouth and talked in her delicate English accent I wanted to pick her up and put her in my mouth, she was so sweet and pretty. We shook hands, she introduced me to her husband who smiled at me from among the paintings, and the lesson began.

At first her tuition frightened me because we only played Bach and he seemed so complicated and different that it took a while before I started to relax. Mrs Massinovitch was very disciplined in the way she taught, very strict, even though everything she wanted me to do was phrased in the politest way possible. In those first lessons it seemed like the only thing she said was, 'You must do it this way Eunice, Bach would like it this way, do it again!' And so I would.

As time went on I began to understand why Mrs Massinovitch only allowed me to practise Bach and soon I loved him as much as she did. He is technically perfect. When you play Bach's music you have to understand that he's a mathematician and all the notes you play add up to something – they make sense. They always add up to climaxes, like ocean waves getting bigger and bigger until after a while when so many waves have gathered you have a great storm. Each note you play is connected to the next note, and every note has to be executed perfectly or the whole effect is lost. Once I understood Bach's music I never wanted to be anything other than a concert pianist; Bach made me dedicate my life to music, and it was Mrs Massinovitch who introduced me to his world. I had set out on a journey which became more wonderful and thrilling each week.

Within a couple of months Mrs Massinovitch and I became firm friends. I called her 'Miz Mazzy', and she found every Saturday morning as enjoyable as I did. It wasn't all hard work, either – we had fun too.

Miz Mazzy kept a big basket of candy on top of the piano, full to the brim. About an hour after the start of the lesson we would have a break. I got to choose a piece of candy from the basket and we moved off the grand piano – which was for serious practice only – and over to the upright piano by the wall, where we played duets together – bright, funny pieces that came as a welcome relief.

My mornings in that house were spent in the company of some of the greatest men that have ever lived, and we talked about them and their music as if they were actually there with us and had just slipped out of the room for a moment.

In summer Miz Mazzy would give me a glass of lemonade and we'd sit talking together in the sunlight looking out into the garden while I finished my candy. When winter came, a great log fire burned in the fireplace and Miz Mazzy would complain that the house was too cold: 'Uninhabitable Eunice. Simply uninhabitable!' The exact same words every winter, forgotten every spring.

Soon she became openly affectionate and occasionally kissed me, or stroked my hair while she was talking. She gave me the kind of attention and affection that I didn't get from Momma, and the more she gave the more I needed it. She had no children of her own, and I was sharing Momma with the rest of the family and the Methodist Church. Maybe in a way we both needed each other in order to fill the gaps in our lives. In time she became another mother to me, one I had all to myself. That was how I came to think of her, as my white momma.

It seemed like I had only begun to learn a fraction of what Miz Mazzy could teach me before the year of lessons that Mrs Miller paid for was over and a decision had to be made about the future. Kind as she was, Mrs Miller couldn't afford to sponsor me forever; and as far as the lack of money at home was concerned, nothing had changed. When she saw the situation Miz Mazzy took command and decided that I needed a secure musical future. If my family wasn't able to provide it, then the town would. And that was what happened. Miz Mazzy founded the Eunice Waymon Fund, a fund to which everybody in Tryon could contribute and which would ensure my musical education not just for the next year but for as long as it was needed.

Miz Mazzy set about raising money with the same dedication that she put into our mornings at the piano. She wrote to the local paper explaining the situation and asking for donations. She talked about me to her friends and got them involved in fund-raising too. Before long everyone in town knew about me and they all did what they could. Every church took up a collection for the Fund, the paper started an appeal and the council collected on my behalf. I became well known; white folks would point to me on the street and call me 'Mrs Massinovitch's little coloured girl'. And so I was, although I didn't like the way they said it.

The Fund money paid for my tuition each week, and any extra was put away for the future. All the people who gave to the Fund had a natural interest in how I was coming along, so part of the deal was that I gave regular recitals at a hall in town so they could come and hear for themselves. Miz Mazzy had always included technical training in my lessons, like how to hold my hands at the keyboard, how to play from the shoulder rather than the wrist and how to improve the spread of my fingers, but now that I was to perform in public a whole new set of disciplines started. My lessons included practising how to bow after a recital, how to walk gracefully on and off stage, and how to sit up straight at the piano and look elegant and composed while I was being introduced.

I had my first piano lesson when I was six and a half and they continued non-stop until I was twelve and left for high school. So that was five and a half years with Miz Mazzy. The Fund started when I was seven and a half, and I was about eight years old when I gave my first public recital. At the same time I was playing in church, just like I had since I was six, and going out on the road with Momma. So I was a busy child, hardly stopping to catch my breath. All the time there was the weight of my community's expectations on my shoulders.

At home the old rules applied: don't get big-headed, don't push yourself forward, thank the Lord. But outside it was different: white folks I never met before came up to me in the drugstore and patted me on my head. I was being trained by Miz Mazzy for public appearances, and all the time I felt the pride in my community that it was a black girl who was being written about in the newspaper and getting all the attention. But at home it was as if none of that was happening, and the faster I progressed with Miz Mazzy the further away I seemed to get from my parents. Music had become such a serious business for me all of a sudden. There was a lot of black pride and money invested in me, and a fair amount of white money too. No matter what they said at home I knew I wasn't like everybody else, I wasn't like them any more.

Daddy and I were still pals, but I didn't have the time to spend with him that I did before all the fuss started. He was busier, too. His health was much better and in 1939 he got a full-time job five miles away in Landrum, working as a foreman in a dry-cleaning plant.

By the time war broke out we had moved to a big house with a wide porch at the back and a large garden. Lucille was going to get married shortly, and Carrol and Harold were old enough for Daddy to hope the war would end before Carrol had to do his army service. All that time ago when I was talking to Daddy about Harold I had said that we were a black family and we had to move fast; and now it was true – we were really moving.

More and more of my life was spent away from the close confines of my home – at school, church, or Miz Mazzy's – and as I became more independent and removed from the protection of my family I became aware that there were things going on all around me that I had never noticed before. Sometimes they were so obvious I couldn't understand why I'd gone for so long without remarking on them, like not being able to sit down at Owen's Pharmacy or not being able to use the bathroom at gas stations on the way back from backwoods revival meetings. Other times they were more puzzling: one day Mrs Miller simply stopped bringing David around to play, and when I was at her house he was discouraged from playing with me; we had crossed an invisible boundary which neither of us understood. Somehow it had been decided that we were both now too old to play as if the colour of our skins made no difference. One of John Irvine's friends left town overnight and the story went round that he'd been seeing a white girl. All the adults nodded wisely as if that was all right – they understood. Understood *what*, I wanted to know.

When I was eleven years old I was asked to give a recital in the town hall. I sat at the piano with my trained elegance while a white man introduced me, and when I looked up my parents, who were dressed in their best, were being thrown out of their front row seats in favour of a white family I had never seen before. And Daddy and Momma were allowing themselves to be moved. Nobody else said anything, but I wasn't going to see them treated like that and stood up in my starched dress and said if anyone expected to hear me play then they'd better make sure that my family was sitting right there in the front row where I could see them, and to hell with poise and elegance. So they moved them back. But my parents were embarrassed and I saw some of the white folks laughing at me.

All of a sudden it seemed a different world, and nothing was easy any more. I really had thought that all white people were like Miz Mazzy and Mrs Miller, all kind and elegant, all polite. I had no reason to think otherwise: they were the only white people I had ever talked to for any length of time. But now prejudice had been made real for me and it was like switching on a light.

I started to think about the way I felt when I walked over to Miz Mazzy's house and crossed the railtrack into the white district. I took to stopping in the drugstore to observe the mixture of indifference and disdain that I provoked in the white customers. The day after the recital I walked around feeling as if I had been flayed and every slight, real or imagined, cut me raw. But the skin grew back again a little tougher, a little less innocent, and a little more black.

Chapter 3

That year, as I took my first steps towards adulthood, the news of the end of the war in Europe was announced. Daddy and Carrol seemed to think it important, but it meant less to me than the radio soap operas I listened to everyday. Carrol was in uniform by then, stationed in Virginia near one of our uncles. Lucille was married, living in Philadelphia with a family of her own.

Momma hadn't finished either: my youngest sister, Frances, was born in April 1942, and my brother Sam in the middle of 1944. But their arrival couldn't fill the gap that Lucille's going left. I'd always known she'd leave to get married one day no matter how much I hoped it wouldn't happen, or prayed a tree would fall on her intended. Sure enough, when the right man came along Lucille moved to the city. John Irvine was gone too, and I never knew why. It was enough to know he felt he couldn't stay at home any longer, and once he left I never saw him again for seventeen years. To this day I don't know what passed between him and my father, but I saw how Daddy was when he was in pain, how he kept his feelings close to his heart and lived alone with his hurt. He never talked about how he felt about losing his eldest son, which is what John Irvine's going amounted to. Among the rest of us it was simply accepted and left alone.

The house we lived in after John Irvine and Lucille had gone wasn't particularly comfortable – the cracked wooden floors let the wind through and the doors didn't sit well in their frames – but it had three bedrooms, a closed-off area at the end of the back porch which could make a fourth, a great wood stove in the kitchen that heated up the bathwater every Saturday night, and a water tap in the kitchen. It was the first time we had lived in a house with running water. Structurally the house was similar to our first home, the one by the tennis court, and for my parents it was proof that after the Depression and Daddy's illness things were getting back to the way they were. I remember it most of all as the house where we grew up, where it seemed like I turned around for a moment and when I looked back the brothers and sisters I had played with were gone, replaced by soldiers, college students, young mothers and in John Irvine's case, nothing but empty space.

Dorothy grew up fast and pretty – too pretty to wear the strapless gown she had chosen for her graduation. Momma came down on the side of the teachers and, although Dorothy swore she'd die if she wasn't allowed to wear that dress, she survived. Harold didn't have to go into the army, so he went off to college; he caused a sensation the first time he came home, when he walked in with a grin on his face and his hair dyed bright red. Momma was mortified and declared he wasn't allowed to accompany her to church looking like he did. Harold didn't mind that enough to wash the henna out.

In 1943 Daddy quit working in the dry-cleaning business and started jobbing around town, as a kind of handyman. I'm not sure why he gave up his steady job; I think once he saw the family back on track and the older children on their way he decided to take some time for himself. Over the years his struggles had damn near killed him: Daddy knew how much harder things were because he was black but he never mentioned it to anyone, and the spirit he had, the desire to achieve on his own merits, never left him.

In fact he was prepared to suffer in order to be his own man. He was reduced for a while to gardening for white folks, hauling wood, fixing their fences. Sometimes he waited on table for those same families when they had fancy dinner parties, standing with a napkin on his arm spooning out potatoes to strangers, wondering just how slavish he should be to get a big tip. And Momma – an ordained minister, a renowned preacher, a delegate to the American Methodist Church Convention in Atlanta, all that and more – worked with him. After forty-five years of believing that if he worked hard and trusted in God then, black man or not, he would advance in society, Daddy was reduced to acting the friendly black butler, like the ones we saw in the Hollywood movies every Saturday morning at Tryon's (segregated) picture house.

Maybe Daddy knew things could have been different and that he lost his chance somewhere along the way. It would explain a few things. Maybe John Irvine knew it too, and said something about it –

29

something that Daddy could not let be spoken aloud, so he banished him forever. In time I too would come to know that there were some things Daddy's pride would not allow him to face.

In the meantime he still had the energy and imagination to try something new, so he built a small extension on the side of the house, bought in some stock and opened a little store. He sold candy and foodstuffs and got up early in the morning to make sandwiches which he sold to men on their way to work. He'd go out at lunchtimes too, selling food out of the back of his car – the same old Ford after all those years. There was no question that his pride was hurt by the fact that Momma and the older children were the ones who provided much of the income that kept our family going. It made no difference that it wasn't his fault, that he had done nothing wrong. He felt he'd let us down, and it burnt inside him. At times there was a lot of conflict between Daddy and his children, like with John Irvine. And conflict between Daddy and Momma, too, which all came out of this frustration Daddy felt.

For myself, I began to look at my parents more critically. Part of this had to do with the resentment I felt that no one in the family knew how isolated my music made me. With my hours at the piano I didn't see friends that much, and when I did all they wanted was for me to play while they danced. At home Momma didn't seem too interested in what I was doing; after making plans for lessons and showing me off in the community and making me play for her in church before her services, she didn't seem to care how I was coming along inside, as a person. That hurt. Momma had always been a little like that, a little detached, but it stood out when I walked into Miz Mazzy's and she wrapped her arms around me and I experienced an affection I didn't get at home. I started to make comparisons. I couldn't recall the last time Momma had taken me into her arms, or kissed me, or told me she was proud of me. Being around Miz Mazzy only brought that home harder: I saw how happy she was with her husband, how she lived to die for him, and I thought about Momma and Daddy, who were very different together. My family wasn't so perfect any more and a gap opened up between us, between Momma and me, that would get larger as time went by.

The fact that my talent stood me apart from my family and friends was something that I would just have to get used to – I knew that even then; but my loneliness was exaggerated because of all the girls

I hung round with I was the only one without a boyfriend. There had been one boy at school I really liked, but he didn't want to know. Naturally I started to think that there was something wrong with me. I was already shy, and watching my friends get picked off one by one until I was left, alone, convinced me I was some kind of freak. Pressure was building inside me from home, school, Momma, music and Miz Mazzy. One afternoon I was with Daddy in the car, going into town on some errand. Daddy said a new family by the name of Whiteside had moved into the house on top of the hill. I looked out and saw a boy, aged about fourteen, standing in their yard. He was the new folks' son, named Edney, I was told.

I wanted him from the moment I saw him. I might not have been able to say exactly what I felt when I looked over at Edney but I knew that whatever it was, I wanted more. I just looked at him and got torn up. The Whitesides were Cherokee Indians and looking at Edney I realized why people called them Red. His skin was a rich ochre and it glowed like there was a light behind it, always. All the Whitesides had black hair which hung straight and beautiful, but Edney's was like his grandmother's, shining and full. He was a little taller than me, and handsome, with great brown eyes tinged with olive. I watched him carefully for a few days and he seemed to be alone most of the time. He was too old to go to school and he hung around the yard, fixing things up for his parents as they settled in.

Edney was shy too, and so although he was just as interested in me as I was in him, we circled around darting glances when we each thought the other wasn't looking, neither saying a word, until one Sunday morning he came up to me after church and asked if he could walk me home. He could have rolled me home in a barrel if he wanted. Soon we were boyfriend and girlfriend, and would stay so until I was seventeen. He smelt wonderful, better than any other man I have ever known, and getting next to him, leaning my head on his shoulder as we sat in his car, gave me real physical pleasure long before we kissed or touched each other.

We met at four in the afternoon every Sunday on an official date. From the moment we started going together our families approved, and everyone assumed that one day we would get married. It seemed like destiny. On Sundays we'd get into his dark green Chevrolet and drive up to Edneyville, the town he was named from, to see his grandmother. She lived in a small house next to a peach orchard, and

31

after visiting her we'd sit in the Chevy to talk. As the sun went down over the mountains I'd run my fingers through his hair, the car would smell sweet with a mixture of peaches and Edney, and I hardly dared kiss him for fear of starting something I wouldn't have the will to stop.

Among the women who had done so much to decide the direction of my life – Momma, Miz Mazzy and Mrs Miller – a great debate was going on as to the next move for their prodigy. Miz Mazzy taught piano to children up to a certain age and then passed them on, and she knew there was a limit to what she could teach and that I would need more specialized tution. The Eunice Waymon Fund was still going strong and a high school had to be decided on, but first they had to decide what my musical prospects were and how my talent could be developed in the right way.

Miz Mazzy's ambition had always been for me to become a classical concert pianist. Momma's too: she wanted me to become the first black American concert pianist. It was ironic that Momma's ambition was so tied to race when she spent the whole of her life trying to ignore the reality of her colour. At home we never talked about race, ever. It was the great unspoken that we lived with but never brought out into the open. Over the years Miz Mazzy made it clear that music would lead me to great things, and encouraged me by saying it. That wasn't Momma's way; she had a special gift when it came to letting the family know what she wanted. Without anyone being aware of her saying anything specific, her wishes became known. That's what happened to me. She never said outright that colour had anything to do with her ambitions, but I knew it all the same.

So Miz Mazzy wanted me to have the best music tuition possible, Momma wanted me to receive the social training a black pioneer would need in order not to let down her race, and Mrs Miller wanted me to have a normal life that offered a chance of personal happiness. The answer they decided on was fifty miles from Tryon, in Asheville: the Allen High School for Girls.

Allen High was morally upright, had a good academic record and Mrs Joyce Carrol, a woman who had Miz Mazzy's respect, was piano tutor. It was a private school and fairly advanced, which meant that black pupils were accepted if they could pay the fees. All the teachers were white and the students wore neat starched uniforms and were chaperoned at all times. It was a protected environment, very protected. When Momma and Miz Mazzy told me about it the idea of living away from home didn't bother me. My parents wanted me to do it and I wasn't going to disobey them, and although I knew I'd miss Edney he promised to visit me every Sunday and we both had this unshakeable faith that once I finished school I'd come back to Tryon and we'd get married. I might have been experiencing strong feelings for Edney, I might have felt increasingly separated from my family, I might have lost my closest friend when Lucille went to Philadelphia, but I was still an obedient child and if everyone wanted me to go to school in Asheville then I'd go – and enjoy it.

Enjoying life at Allen High wasn't hard. For the first time in my life I had my own bedroom, and I loved that. I made friends quickly – Patricia Carlson and Dorothy McLure, friends who lived near Tryon – and in the holidays we'd call each other up and go to sleep over at each other's houses. It was good to be in the company of other girls all the time; we'd talk about boys and music, play games, go out to the movies together and when we had time teach each other how to jitterbug or hully-gully.

It was all very innocent: we were respectable young ladies who never dreamed of breaking out of our delicate shells. Every now and then we got a little taste of the outside world, like when Irma Wesley started talking about boys one day, but not in the way we normally did. She said the boys she knew were just about full-grown men and went on to describe stuff that made our eyes bug out. Elise Blanc said that Irma's talk was shameful and she wasn't going to listen to it any more, so out she flounced. I stayed, and realized that no matter how grown-up Edney made me feel I was very young compared to Irma. Next day I asked Patricia how come Irma knew so much about boys, and she looked at me like I was a simpleton. 'She's from Louisiana,' she said, explaining everything.

Lessons were easy, I got straight As and the teachers were as kind to me as Mrs McKissick was back home. Music was still the constant: I had lessons with Mrs Carrol twice a week and practised every day, practised hard. I got up at four in the morning, before anyone else, and played until eight. In all I averaged around five hours a day at the piano the whole time I was in High School. I was pianist for the glee club and played for the school orchestra as well as in church on Sundays, which meant choir practice during the week.

It was hard work, but Miz Mazzy had shown me how good it could be to spend time in the company of genius, so the more familiar I became with Mozart and Beethoven, Czerny and Liszt, and my beloved Bach, the more I enjoyed it. As I grew older I had a sense that my future was as much in my own hands as in those of my teachers – that they pointed me in various musical directions, but I was doing the exploring on my own.

When I went home in the holidays I'd walk through Gilette Woods to Miz Mazzy's and she'd sit quietly as I played to her, not showing off but showing where I was going. Over the years she corrected my playing less and less and sat listening more and more. And when I'd finished we'd move over to the upright by the wall and play duets, like always.

During termtime Edney drove the fifty miles from Tryon every Sunday. We met at four – me with my chaperone – for an hour or so. Back home we had seen each other nearly every day so our separation was difficult at first, and because of the chaperone there were a lot of longing glances and meaningful silences when we did get together. Edney wrote every week and I devoured his letters. I wouldn't show them to my friends because he couldn't spell worth a damn, but getting them was enough for me no matter how they read. At home in the holidays the two of us would sit and talk about our wedding, where we would live and so on. This wasn't kids' fantasy; I was coming up to sixteen and Edney was two years older than me so we were easily old enough. We both knew kids younger than us who were married.

By now Edney and I had left innocent kissing far behind. One summer he went to Youngstown, Ohio for a few weeks and came back wearing a new suit, looking as good as I had ever seen him. I wasn't the only one who noticed, and it struck me that whispered promises of what was to come might not be enough to keep my man interested. I didn't blame him, because I wanted to make love as much as he did – I'd wanted to since I was twelve years old. The question disturbed me: if Edney and I were going to marry anyway, why couldn't we make love now? Daddy – no fool – told me to ask Momma. So I did. She said what you would expect a mother to say, and after she told Mrs Whiteside of our conversation Edney got told the same in stronger language. That was the end of it. We were obedient children, to my eternal regret.

I went back to school and Edney's letters started to get less frequent. Then he missed a Sunday visit, so I went home to see him the next weekend. He told me he was seeing a good friend of mine, Annie Mae. The way he put it was so simple, 'Yes, I'm going with her, you're not home. You're not home and I miss you too much.'

There was nothing to say. I did my crying back in Asheville. I was in my graduation year and things were going crazy. I practised all hours I could because it was the only way I could stop thinking about Edney. I studied like a demon because I wanted to graduate Valedictorian, top of my year. When I went home there were endless conversations about the future, which, without Edney, I cared nothing about.

Although it might seem like a juvenile affair, Edney and I were a lot more than that. We weren't giddy teenagers, we were the children of poor families who worked hard to move up and who knew one piece of bad luck could send a whole family spinning back down into poverty. Our parents didn't want us to get married just because we looked cute together; it made sense to them for all sorts of reasons, romantic and economic. And I knew how lonely music made me, how I couldn't talk about it to anyone and how the hours I devoted to it stopped me from having a normal life. In Tryon and even in my family, as I grew older, I was regarded as an exception, as not like them. I was out on my own. In Edney, whom I loved and who loved me, I had someone to connect with, to tie me to the real world, to love more than music.

I was due to graduate in June 1950. At the end of May Edney told me he was coming to my graduation and bringing his mother and father. Although he was still seeing Annie Mae and I had heard a rumour they were going to be married, he explained her away by saying that he had to have someone near him. I understood what he meant: if I came home after graduation we would be married. But I'd graduated Valedictorian and had the choice of two scholarships, one of them to the Juilliard School of Music in New York, and Momma and Miz Mazzy had worked out a plan. The Juilliard scholarship was just for a year, but they decided I would use it to prepare for the scholarship examination to the Curtis Institute of Music in Philadelphia. Mrs Miller wanted me to attend a regular college because she thought I needed some music-free time to balance out what I had already given up to practice. She was right, but the lure of the Curtis Institute was too powerful for Momma and Miz Mazzy.

So Commencement came around in June and I gave the Valedictorian's speech and posed for my graduation photograph in a beautiful long gown. Edney and his parents sat with my family, Miz Mazzy and Mrs Miller. He already had an idea what the older folks wanted, and listening to Momma and Miz Mazzy outlining their plans confirmed it. We walked together after the ceremony and talked. He said, 'If you go to New York you won't ever come back. We both know that. So if we don't get married now it will never happen, and if you go I'll marry your best friend.' That's what it came down to. On one side was music, Miz Mazzy, my family, all those long hours of practice and the aspirations of the town I was born in and of my race as well, of my own people. On the other side was Edney, all alone.

We didn't have a chance, either of us. Back home in Tryon a few days later I told him that I was going to New York. He didn't say anything, just pushed me backwards and tried to kiss me, tried to force himself on me, tried to make love to me, as if he saw all those years of self-control laid out behind him to no purpose. In some way he was trying to rape me, but it wasn't frightening or dangerous – it was sad and funny at the same time. I laughed as he grabbed on to me, not understanding that he was trying to keep me there any way he could, including by force. He couldn't do it – he didn't know how because he wasn't a brute, he was a sensitive beautiful man and he couldn't do it and I laughed and laughed until he jumped up and walked away.

I left for New York and Edney married Annie Mae and they moved into his father's house. I had given Edney a copy of my graduation photograph and he and Annie Mae kept it on their piano. Nobody was allowed to touch it.

Over the next few years when I came back to Tryon to visit my family I'd meet Mrs Whiteside, Edney's mother, and she'd say: 'Why didn't you come get my boy? Why didn't you come get my boy?' And I'd say something like; 'Well, maybe I'll be back in a couple of years.' She'd look at me; 'You've got to come get him, Eunice, you're my girl. You've got to come get Edney.'

Later I was having some success in New York and when I was back in Tryon again she saw me and said; 'Take him this time, take him, take Edney.' Then my family moved away from Tryon, and the only reason I went back was to visit Miz Mazzy and try and catch a look at him. I'd see him across the street, sometimes just the back of his head. I talked to him once, about eight years after he married Annie

Mae. I asked him why he did it.

'It was a fool's thing to do,' he said, 'but I was young, and didn't know enough not to marry for spite.'

We looked at each other.

'What did we do wrong?' I asked him.

'We waited,' he said.

Time passed. I travelled all over the world, lived a life I could never have imagined and knew all sorts of love. One day I found myself in Tryon again, alone. I was miserable, and it seemed like God was punishing me for leaving Edney all those years ago. So I decided to claim him at last. I dressed in red, green and black, put on an Yves St Laurent hat and set out. I had my car stop at his house and walked up to the door. Two of his five children stood on the doorstep. They were gigantic. 'Where's your Daddy?' I asked them.

They pointed to the basement. I went down, passing Mrs Whiteside on the stairs, the same woman that had begged me to come find her son so many times. I looked at her and said: 'I've come to get him, Mrs Whiteside.' Two more of his children were at the bottom of the staircase, even bigger than the two at the door. They pointed at a chair in the corner of the room, and there he was.

When I looked at him the rest of the room disappeared. All I saw was a shadow, a man broken by hard work and not enough fun, a skeleton in a weakened body. He was only forty-six years old. I put my hands out to touch his face. 'What on God's earth have they done to you?' I whispered. Then I held him close for around a minute until he remembered his children watching and pulled away. Time stopped for a while. I told him that I was staying over at Miz Mazzy's and I needed to see him, so he should call me. Then I left.

The next morning the phone rang. It was Edney's mother, saying, 'Now Eunice, you waited too long to come for Edney. Every single time I asked you to come get my boy you wouldn't do it, and now it's too late. What happened last night can't happen any more.'

I knew she was right, that he had a life and children he couldn't escape from, but I cried all the same. I asked her about my photograph, and she told me that it was where it had always been, on the piano. I was hurt so much I said, 'Well, it won't be of any value to you now, will it?'

She said that they'd had it for twenty-eight years, but that made no difference to me at that moment.

'Can I have it back?' I said.

Mrs Whiteside agreed that if I called round that evening at ten and sat outside in my car she would bring it to me.

All our years of missed opportunity were in that photograph of me in blue with my hair in bangs, styled in a flip and looking so pretty I couldn't stand myself. All those wasted years. That night I sat in the car as instructed and his mother brought it out. She said, 'I'm not telling Edney and I'm not telling Granddaddy where it went.' And I said, 'If this is the end then I definitely want it.'

She passed it through the window into the limousine and we drove away. I couldn't see my young face in the photograph through the tears. I remembered Edney's favourite song, 'My Happiness', and I sang it in my head – 'Evening shadows make me blue, when each weary day is through. How I long to be with you, My Happiness.'

That was our song. I lost the photograph soon afterwards. I think I left it at Duke Ellington's house. Years later I was sitting on the beach in Barbados having a good time with some friends when I heard 'My Happiness' coming out of a little transistor radio. I cried like a baby all over again, and nothing my friends said could stop the tears.

But those tears were half a lifetime away that summer of my graduation, and when I left for New York I still had the hope that somehow, some way, Edney and I would end up together. With my place at Juilliard arranged, Momma's next problem was finding somewhere for me to live, and she made sure that I would be safe from the evil temptations of the city by calling a preacher friend of hers, Mrs Steinermayer, who agreed to let me stay with her while I studied. She lived in Harlem, on 145th Street, in a house with a wide front porch and a swing chair where you could sit fanning yourself in the evening and watch the world go by.

At first Harlem scared me with its noise – it seemed like no one ever went to sleep at night – but after a while I began to venture out a little way from the house, always in the daytime, to explore. The first day I walked out I turned a corner and there was a group of men drinking and cursing, out there in the street. I was shocked – horrified that people behaved like that where everyone could see them. On the other hand there were all the different food stores, each with their own smell and their windows piled high with things I had never seen before. I was astounded by how beautifully dressed Harlem women were, sashaying down the sidewalk at midday in their coloured silks and hats. Although I was only seventeen and a little innocent I knew how some of these sharp-looking ladies earned a living, but looking at them in their finery I passed no judgement at all. It seemed like a fine life as far as I could tell.

But Harlem wasn't all smoky dives full of gamblers, whores and jazzmen. Mrs Steinermayer had ladies boarding at her house who were perfectly respectable, and they were just as beautiful and sophisticated as any of the women out on the street. I only had one dress that I felt was elegant enough to wear in Harlem and I wore it the whole time I was there, so that by the time I came to leave it was thinner than a spider's web after all the washing I had given it. One evening I sat on the far end of the porch listening to the other ladies talking – these pretty, pretty women hatching plans about the men they were going to marry. The male sensations around Harlem at that time were Sidney Poitier and Coley Wallace, who was a fighter. The ladies sat giggling in the dark with their friends, discussing men in general and those two in particular and I remember one, the prettiest, sitting up and saying; 'Well, I'm going to marry Sidney Poitier.'

Quick as a flash her friend replied, 'Is that so? Well, I'm going to marry Coley Wallace.'

And they did too, although I'd left New York by the time they did and never got to meet either of their targets on my first visit to the city. Back then I sat quietly in my little green dress and marvelled that women only a couple of years older than me could be so grown up, so sophisticated, so sexy.

Mrs Steinermayer and her boarders were the only people I got to know well while I was in New York. I was so shy that making new friends was impossible. I walked around the two or three blocks by my house just looking around, never daring to open my mouth. I had my lessons at Juilliard and I went to the school every day to practise. My tutor was Dr Carl Friedburg, a great teacher, very gifted. I was the only black student he had, but nobody made any mention of it and the fact was of no interest to me. Lessons with Dr Friedberg were a joy because, although they took the same shape as the lessons I'd always had, he was the greatest musician I had met up to that time and I learned something new each time I sat down to play for him.

Every week I played a piece for him to criticize. His corrections were so subtle and delicate that individually each one seemed to make hardly any difference at all, but when I played the piece again afterwards with all his alterations included it shone like polished silver. Studying under Dr Friedberg gave me a satisfaction and happiness I couldn't explain, but I knew this was what I was born to do, what all those hours of practice had been about, and it was leading to my destiny, the classical concert stage.

I learned too that, even at the highest level, lessons that Miz Mazzy had taught me when I was seven years old still had a place. Dr Friedberg and I went through exercises together at the piano and he taught me different techniques to improve my finger, knuckle, wrist, elbow and back movement. It was like being back in that thick-walled house in Tryon with the smell of paint and flowers all around and the dish of candy on top of the piano.

Under Dr Friedberg's careful tuition I began to prepare for the scholarship examination to the Curtis Institute in Philadelphia, my next step as decided by the Tryon ladies on my graduation day. Even though I had won a scholarship to Juilliard I still had to pay twenty-five dollars a week towards lessons and the Fund money was limited, so a full scholarship to Curtis was vital. I visited my old tutors, Mrs Joyce Carrol and Miz Mazzy, and they helped me prepare with a mixture of pride and love. My year in New York was coming to an end, and as the day of the Curtis examination approached I knew I was going to be ready – that I would be able to do my best.

Philadelphia was becoming important not just to me but to my whole family. Carrol finished his army service in 1950 and decided to live in Philadelphia, where one of our uncles had settled. It was obvious to Carrol that there was no point in coming back to the south because work was scarce; and anyhow life was easier for a black man in Philadelphia than it was in North Carolina. Of course this wasn't a fact known only to Carrol, there were many black families in the south after the war who figured a move north was a good idea economically, socially and any other way you cared to look at it.

Back in Tryon my family still relied on Momma to bring in the money to keep them going; of the older children only Dorothy was at home, so there wasn't as much money coming in from the children as before. All those years ago the reason Daddy and Momma had moved to Tryon in the first place was because it offered the best chance of providing enough money to enable the family to educate and improve itself. In a way Tryon had provided much of what Daddy had hoped for: Carrol and Harold had graduated from college, Dorothy and

Lucille from high school, I was at music school in New York and, although times had been hard along the way, none of us had starved. Now there was a feeling in the family that Tryon had run its course for the Waymons, and if we stayed there too much longer things might start to turn down. Philadelphia was where we had family, where Carrol was settling, where Lucille lived and where – it was assumed – I would study music. The decision for the whole family to move to Philly was taken.

Momma moved up in September 1950 and took Frances and baby Sam with her. Daddy stayed down in Tryon for a while to sort everything else out and because we didn't have enough money to move all in one go. It was a sensible arrangement and we children were also aware that things hadn't been too good between Daddy and Momma for a while, so the idea of a forced separation for a period was convenient. I came down to Philadelphia late in the year to take the scholarship examination to Curtis, and then returned to New York to continue my studies under Dr Friedberg for as long as possible. Finally I returned to Philadelphia to see my family. Before long I heard from the Curtis Institute. They didn't want me because I wasn't good enough. Rejected.

I was born into a small community that saw me as an infant and predicted great things. I was raised in a family that watched me perform prodigious musical feats and told me to be thankful that I had been chosen as special by God. I was taken up by strangers – black and white – and adopted as their own. The direction of my life was determined by their ambitions and their money and I was promised a future I had no part in choosing. In return for this great act of faith by everyone I ever knew I applied myself with dedication and turned my back on everything but the fulfillment of our destiny. It was the only thing I knew how to do.

I had no arrogance in regard to my talent, it just never occurred to me that what had been promised would not come about. When I was rejected by the Curtis Institute it was as if all the promises ever made to me by God, my family and my community were broken and I had been lied to all my life. I just couldn't believe it had happened, and all I could think about was what I had given up over the years to get to where I was the day I heard Curtis didn't want me, which was nowhere. It was so hard to understand.

The truth was very simple: in the real world things don't always

41

turn out the way you think they will, and there's nothing you can do about it. But I knew nothing of the real world because I had been sheltered from it for my entire life. The second astonishing thing was how other people didn't understand why I was so destroyed: Momma said maybe I should get a job and keep the music going in my spare time, but how in the name of God was I going to be the first black classical concert pianist – which she had always told me was what I was going to be – in my spare time?

It was the end of everything. The Fund money was almost all gone. Now that I had been rejected why should anyone want to pay out money to a failure?

When I started to think straight there was only one course that I could follow, which was to work twice as hard – if that was possible – and take the Curtis examination again the following year. I ran the idea round in my head but before I got very far with it Carrol came home one night with news. What he said changed everything.

Marion Anderson was one of the great heroes of my family; we all adored this great diva and remembered Independence Day 1939 when, because of the colour of her skin, she was refused entry to Constitution Hall in Washington and so gave her concert on the steps outside to an audience of thousands, including Mrs Roosevelt, the First Lady. She had faced discrimination all her life – not least in Philadelphia, where she spent a lot of time. My uncle Walter was a great friend of hers and over the fifty years he had lived in Philly he had got to know a wide range of people who kept him well informed about the way things worked in the city.

It had never occurred to me to wonder how many black students there were studying at the Curtis Institute: it was a question I should have asked. The story that Carrol heard through my uncle and his friends, black and white, was that the Institute wanted to enrol black students, but if blacks were going to be admitted then they were not going to accept an unknown black, that if they were to accept an unknown black then it was not going to be an unknown black girl, and if they were going to admit an unknown black girl it wasn't going to be a very poor unknown black girl. People who knew – I was told – white people who knew, said the reason I was turned down was because I was black.

The wonderful thing about this type of discrimination is that you can never know for sure if it is true, because no one is going to turn around and admit to being a racist. They just say no, you got turned down because you weren't good enough and you'll never know. So you feel the shame, humiliation and anger at being just another victim of prejudice and at the same time there's the nagging worry that maybe it isn't that at all, maybe it's because you're just no good. More and more people stopped by to tell me 'the real reason you didn't get in to Curtis.' If enough people tell you something often enough, you come to believe them: I wasn't at that stage yet, but I was getting there. One thing was for sure: I was finished with music.

Chapter 4

When Curtis turned me down I was changed forever. When Mrs Miller had paid for my piano lessons and Miz Mazzy started the Fund I had seen it as the rich helping the poor, like Christian people were supposed to do.

The questions I might have asked, like why it was always black women like Momma who cleaned the houses for white people like Mrs Miller, I never did. I knew prejudice existed, but I never thought it could have such a direct affect on my future. Nobody told me that no matter what I did in life the colour of my skin would always make a difference. I learned that bitter lesson from Curtis.

To get away from music I took a job as an assistant in a photographer's darkroom and found I enjoyed the stupid monotony of the work: I just had to lift film in and out of different solutions each time a bell rang. It left me free to think about anything that came into my head. I was a stranger to the piano. Momma was pleased; at least I was doing something instead of sitting around saying nothing like I'd done for days after the news from Curtis came through.

In a way I included Momma in the bitterness I felt, because she turned aside from all the plans we'd made. It was God's will that I failed as a musician and would spend the rest of my life working for peanuts, just as it had been God's will that I should waste my childhood preparing for this humiliation. At least that's how I thought she saw it, and the fact that Momma had experienced terrible disappointments before and her instinct was to put them behind her and get on with the future didn't occur to me. I was too innocent.

Carrol had an older head, and he kept saying I had to get back to serious study, and if we tried hard enough the money could be got somehow – there was always a way. He wouldn't give up on it, night after night, and eventually I let myself be persuaded. The real truth was I missed playing too much: with the tiny amount of Fund money left I enrolled as a private pupil with Vladimir Sokhaloff, who would have been my tutor at Curtis. He encouraged me to consider taking the examination again the following year. At first I couldn't stop thinking about what might have been, but after a couple of lessons Professor Sokhaloff said I really should have been a scholarship student and at last I knew for sure how good I was. Once the terrible insecurity of wondering if I had overestimated my talent was gone, my bitterness went too. I was still angry, but it was a healthy anger. I made the decision to get back into music and to find a way, any way, to pay for my studies. I would be the first black classical concert pianist, no matter what.

Somebody told me a local singing teacher needed an accompanist, and I went for the job. The Arlene Smith Studio was a big, dusty room on the first floor of what used to be a furniture warehouse owned by Arlene herself, a white lady. She gave singing lessons to teenagers who couldn't sing and charged their optimistic parents ten dollars an hour for the privilege. She made good money, helped by the fact that she only paid her accompanists a dollar an hour. She had a little room around the corner from the studio where her housekeeper Odessa cooked hot meals for the staff, which was supposed to help make up for the low wages. It didn't, but when Arlene offered the job I took it because at least it had to do with music.

I was a good accompanist. I knew how to improvise and I could play any song in any key, so I made the students sound good – better than they really were – when their parents came to check on them. Another girl, Ingrid, was working there when I arrived, doing the same job as me. She never said much, just chewed gum right through the lessons, blowing huge bubbles as her students struggled through 'My Funny Valentine' or 'Near to You'.

We taught mainly popular songs and standards. The kids loved the latest hits, their parents the old favourites, and we liked anything we hadn't played before – so when they asked us for a song to learn we'd rummage about in our minds (or in the sheet music) for some old show tune nobody had heard of. I didn't know many numbers when I started, but Arlene ran through the most popular ones and I picked up the rest as I went along. I held them in my head rather than use sheet music – it saved time.

Working eight hours a day, five days a week, I earned fifty dollars.

Twenty-five dollars went on my lesson, I gave what I could to Momma and lived off the rest. I practised four or five hours a day outside of work, so I didn't get out too much. I went to church on Sundays and occasionally saw a European film at an art house theatre. I went on Saturday afternoons, usually on my own, but sometimes with a girlfriend. I went with Ingrid one time and her bubbles nearly drove me crazy, so it was only the one time!

Arlene soon trusted me to take lessons unsupervised. The kids were always very uptight in the way they sang – it was a struggle getting them to put any feeling into the lyrics, and I had to sing the words myself to show them how to do it. I never thought much of my voice but I knew how to carry a song without any problem, which was more than most of them could do, and when they tried to copy me it usually sounded a little better than it had before. Working in the studio like that, trying to help some spotty teenager sound like Frank Sinatra, was the first time I ever earned money singing.

It took me a few months to settle down to this life, moving between my own classical training and the studio, but soon I got on top of the routine and decided to find a place of my own. The problem was money. I figured the only way to do it was for me to quit the studio and give private tuition, where I could charge $2.50 an hour. So I quit, set myself up as a private tutor and rented a storefront, which was a studio during the day and my bedroom at night. Arlene wasn't too happy because I took eight of her students with me – at half price compared to her – and things cooled between us. But eventually she forgave me and even offered a little part-time work at the studio, which helped when times were hard.

My storefront on 57th Street and Master was just that, a store that opened out on to the street. The last owners had gone broke and no shop people wanted it, so I got it cheap. I had my own place and my own money to spend – although I still gave some to Momma every week – so I had a lot of fun fixing it up. I made curtains, then bought furniture, pictures, a little phonograph and a few records.

My pupils came during the day, and in the evening when the last of them had gone I'd draw the curtains across and sit at the piano with Sheba, my dog, rubbing against my feet while I prepared my weekly lesson with Vladimir Sokhaloff.

It wasn't an exciting life but I was kind of contented, and if things got a little quiet there was always church to look forward to: sometimes you meet the most interesting people in church.

Ed's mother was a preacher, too. She and Momma were good friends and Ed was a baritone in the choir. The first time I saw him he was singing semi-classics, the sort Daddy liked. He was tall, good-looking and very neat – almost vain. I hadn't gone out with anybody since Edney apart from one brief episode in New York when I'd run into an old friend from North Carolina. We were both missing home and finding Harlem a little too much to deal with, and we'd looked at each other with delight when we met by chance on the street. That day – as ever – I was missing Edney, and this boy, who knew him and was from home, took his place that night.

It wasn't what I expected, not at all. It hurt like hell and put me off the whole idea of men for a good while, but when Ed came up after church one week and asked to walk me home just like Edney had when I was twelve, I said yes. We went back to my storefront and I pulled the curtains across and sent Sheba out to play. When she got back I was purring. I went with Ed for some time and he even talked about getting married, which was when I finished with him. But he taught me a lot: I had never had a real boyfriend all the way through and by the time I finished with Ed I knew I would never be innocent again. The whole time I wished he could have been Edney.

Mostly I was on my own, working hard, practising, isolating myself. I saw very few people, and none of the men I knew in Philadelphia meant anything much to me. I lived like this for almost three years, trying to save enough money to stop working and dedicate myself to music and not getting anywhere near it. I began to feel uneasy because I didn't seem to fit in with any of the people I met; I wasn't making friends. I started seeing a psychiatrist named Gerry Weiss and went to his office for analysis every Thursday for a year. I'd lie on his couch and talk, do free association and stuff. I liked doing it but although Gerry became a friend – so in a way the analysis worked – I didn't feel it was doing me any good, so I stopped.

My only real friend in Philadelphia was a woman named Faith Jackson. Her customers knew her as Kevin Matthias, and she was a whore. I wasn't shocked when she told me that, because seeing those brightly dressed ladies in Harlem had taught me that there was a lot more to the world than Momma would have me believe. I kind of lived through her. I never envy other people's careers or money, I envy their freedom, and I think I was more envious of Kevin than of any woman

I ever knew. She was free, she was beautiful and she could get men all the time. They gave her money and clothes, and what they didn't give her she bought herself – she always wore the most beautiful shoes – and her men did what she wanted or she got rid of them. She had no pimp because she never needed one; she was totally independent and took care of everything herself. I admired her, and she must have seen something to like in me because she gathered me under her wing and took me along to parties sometimes, introducing me to her friends.

I can't remember how we met, but she lived nearby and somehow we just drifted together. That was unusual enough, given how different we were, but life with Kevin could be strange like that. She came round one time to invite me to Christmas dinner at her apartment. When I asked if I should bring anything or would she like some help with the cooking she laughed. On Christmas Day her apartment was spotless. Kevin was stretched out on the sofa, looking elegant. The smell of roast turkey came from the kitchen and a man appeared, took my coat and offered me a drink. Kevin didn't say anything, just smiled. When he went back into the kitchen she explained. He was a john, a customer who paid her to let him cook and serve Christmas dinner. All she had to do was go in every half hour or so and beat him with a whip. I swear this is true. I almost died.

Kevin went to Atlantic City every summer because guys spend money on holiday and she always did good business at resorts. Other Philly people I knew – older kids I taught who were in college – worked down there during the summer when the hotels took on extra staff. Early in 1954 I talked to some of my students about it. Most of them were going to be waiters or bellhops, but one kid said he was going to be working in a bar, playing piano. I looked at him kind of strange, because of all people I was the one to know he couldn't play for beans, but he just grinned back and said, 'Yeah, I know, but they're going to pay me ninety dollars a week.'

I thought about it a while. Ninety dollars was double what I earned and that was just what the bar paid – if the customers liked you there were tips on top. The next time I saw the kid I got the number of his agent and called the guy up. I wasn't nervous, figuring if one of my students could get a job as a pianist, so could I. Sure enough the guy called back and told me I had a job for the summer, at a place called the Midtown Bar and Grill.

The only problem was Momma finding out I was going to be playing piano in a bar. To her that wouldn't be any different from working in the fires of hell. I could already hear her voice in my head: 'A bar? My God, in my own family I have the devil himself!' I couldn't see how Momma would ever find out, but somehow with these sort of things she always did. Anyhow, if there was a sign on the street saying 'Playing Tonight: Eunice Waymon' it would certainly increase the chances, so I decided to use a stage name. I'd had a Hispanic boyfriend one time, Chico, who had christened me Niña, pronounced Neen-ya, which was the Spanish for 'little one'. Chico had called me that all the time, and I really loved the way it sounded. And I liked the name Simone too, ever since I'd seen Simone Signoret in those French movies. So there it was, Nina Simone. I tried it out on Kevin, who said it sounded very sophisticated. So when summer came I left Philly as Eunice Waymon and arrived in Atlantic City as Nina Simone.

The Midtown Bar and Grill was on Pacific Avenue, two blocks back from the seafront boardwalk. I was told to turn up that first night, introduce myself to the owner and play. I found the Midtown and stood on the sidewalk building up the courage to go in. From outside the Midtown looked like nothing at all – just a seedy little bar where old guys go to huddle over a drink and fall asleep. That's exactly what it was.

Up to that moment I had never been into a bar in my entire life. I pushed the door open and my eyes watered from the smoke and my nose twitched as the smell of the place hit me. I walked up to the bar and asked if I could please speak to Harry Steward, the owner. The barman asked what I wanted and I said I was the new pianist. He said Harry was a little tied up, would I wait? I said yes. He asked if I wanted a drink and I asked for a glass of milk. A few of the old Irish guys around the bar laughed. I blushed.

I looked around out of the corner of my eye. The Midtown was just one long room with the bar stretching two-thirds of the way down one wall. Some tables and chairs were laid out in the remaining space, and a piano stood on a tiny raised stage at the back. I reckoned the entire place could hold about a hundred people if you greased each one and slid them in sideways. There was a door by the end of the bar, and behind that was a room where they put the drunks to sleep it off when they'd had too much to make it home. Sawdust on the floor. A joint. No other word for it – at least no decent one.

Harry Steward came out from his room at the back. He was a little

Jewish guy and had a fat cigar in his mouth as a permanent fixture. He took me up to look at the piano – which was OK – and in the roof above the keyboard, exactly over where I would sit, was a leaky air-conditioning machine. Water was dripping down on to the piano stool. Harry went into his office and came out a moment later with a black umbrella which he opened and jammed into the ceiling by the air conditioner so that the water dribbled down the side of the umbrella and fell in a little pool in front of one of the tables. He stuck a bucket on top of the puddle and told me to come back in an hour to start work.

The guys at the bar must have thought I was from another planet when I walked in that night. The only public performances I had ever given were classical recitals, and all my training in presentation was for the concert stage. I decided that whatever they might think of me I was probably the finest pianist they'd ever hear, so I was going to present myself as such. When it came to actually playing I would get through it by closing my eyes and pretending I was somewhere else, like Carnegie Hall or the Metropolitan Opera. So I put on my best long chiffon gown, fixed my make-up and hair just like I always did and went to work.

Nobody said anything when I walked in, but they all turned to look at me. Harry's cigar almost went out. I sat on stage a diva, a professional entertainer for the first time, and played to an audience of drunken Irish bums.

The deal was I performed from 9 p.m. to 4 a.m., with a break of fifteen minutes every hour. For that I got ninety dollars a week plus tips and as much milk as I could drink. That first night the only thing I wasn't nervous about was what to play. I knew hundreds of popular songs and dozens of classical pieces, so what I did was combine them: I arrived prepared with classical pieces, hymns and gospel songs and improvised on those, occasionally slipping in a part from a popular tune. Each song – which isn't the right way to describe what I was playing – lasted anywhere between thirty and ninety minutes. I just sat down, closed my eyes and drifted away on the music.

On my first night, one song I played lasted for three hours without a break. The guys in the bar were used to pianists playing no more than half a dozen tunes in each set and usually repeating the same set over and over. When I played they never heard the same song twice in a night, and when I was really flying they didn't hear the same song once. I used no sheet music because it was all in my head. Between sets I sat on my own at the bar, drinking milk in my long chiffon gown. Nobody said a word to me all night.

So that first evening I closed my eyes and played. Four a.m. came round and they started piling up the drunks in the side room and putting the chairs on the tables, getting ready to close up. Harry was waiting for me at the bar when I finished and I asked him if it had gone all right. He was very nice about my playing, said he liked it, but there was just one thing, why hadn't I sung?

I looked at him. 'I'm only a pianist,' I said.

He took his cigar out of his mouth: 'Well tomorrow night you're either a singer or you're out of a job.'

So the next night I sang as well. It wasn't hard to fit it to the improvisation because I used my voice as a third layer, complementing the other two layers, my right and left hands. When I got to the part where I used elements of popular songs I would simply sing the lyric and play around with it, repeating single lines over again, repeating verses, changing the order of the words. It was fun. Harry liked it too, so everybody was happy.

Before I started at the Midtown Bar my musical life was separated into two halves. The tuition I gave at my storefront was simply a way of earning money to keep up my studies; I didn't even think of it as music – it was just a job. Because I spent so long accompanying untalented students I came to despise popular songs and I never played them for my own amusement – why should I when I could be playing Bach, or Czerny or Liszt? That was real music, and in it I found a happiness I didn't have to share with anybody. So the only way I could stand playing in the Midtown was to make my set as close to classical music as possible without getting fired. This meant I had to include some popular music and I had to sing, which I'd never thought of doing. The strange thing was that when I started to do it, to bring the two halves together, I found a pleasure in it almost as deep as the pleasure I got from classical music. Playing at the Midtown made me looser and more relaxed about music. I was creating something new, something that came out of me.

Because I had to play seven hours a night I started to improvise, but I didn't know I could do it until I had to. When I sat down at the piano on my first night I had no idea of the shape of the music I would play. It just came out without my thinking about it, the first original music I ever played. I was repressed to the point where I hadn't played any of my own songs before because I didn't know I had them down there; I didn't know until they came out. They came out with Bach's technique, but they were my songs, and I wrote new ones every night.

Towards the end of my first week at the Midtown I noticed that, late in the evening, new customers appeared and kept telling the old guys to quieten down while I was playing. Between sets I looked at the audience and saw there were a few younger customers in. The following nights they were there again, always after about 1.30, and they had friends with them who were coming to the Midtown for the first time. Then someone came up and complimented me on my playing. I got a big kick from that, but after a couple of weeks it was unusual if I didn't get complimented. It seemed like I wasn't the only one who was enjoying my music.

I was starting to get a reputation around town, spread through word of mouth by people who had drifted into the Midtown by chance. These people were students working in Atlantic City, and they came late because they didn't finish work until after midnight. A lot of the regular old Irish guys started leaving when the kids arrived, and some stopped coming altogether. Harry didn't mind; the place was fuller than it had been for years. They liked me so much that they'd come in to the Midtown early on their evenings off, and they'd bring their friends.

My attitude to performing was that of a classically trained musician: when you play you give all your concentration to the music because it deserves total respect, and an audience should sit still and be quiet. That's how I played at the Midtown, and my students understood it. If a drunk started shouting or fighting while I was playing, it broke my concentration so I stopped playing until they were quiet, and if they weren't quiet I wouldn't play. When that happened, my students would grab the guy and throw him out on the street. My attitude to live audiences was formed there at the Midtown and it's never changed, no matter who the audience or how big the concert hall. If an audience disrespects me it is insulting the music I play and I will not continue, because if they don't want to listen then I don't want to play. An audience chooses to come and see me perform; I don't choose the audience. I don't need them either, and if they don't like my attitude then they don't have to come and see me. Others will.

Although by the end of the summer there was a whole bunch of the students who came and saw me and who I knew by name, there were hardly any that I would have said were my friends. I was still terribly shy. I would walk home – alone – to my rooming house on Pacific Avenue and fall into bed, sleep for six or seven hours, wake up, sweep out my room and listen to records for most of the day. Kevin would be around sometimes and we'd go out together but she worked long hours too, so often I only had my own company. I think people were wary of me; they watched me perform, playing for hours with my eyes closed, and they thought I was a little strange. I know they did, because one night at the Midtown I overheard someone saying that I was from Lexington, Kentucky and I was a dope addict, which was why I played for hours with my eyes closed – I was high. And I only drank milk because I got sick when I drank liquor. I went back to my room that night and cried for hours at the idea that people were going around saying that about me.

When summer ended I went back to my storefront in Philadelphia and became Eunice Waymon once more. My lessons with Vladimir Sokhaloff resumed without any problem, but teaching students really started to get me down. I began to think about playing live again – not because I enjoyed it that much, but it was easier, and paid more. It struck me that if I were a little more successful as a performer I could give up private tuition altogether and save enough to study at a music conservatory full time – possibly even go back to Juilliard for a couple of years.

I returned to Atlantic City the following summer with that in mind. At the Midtown I picked up where I left off and the bar was full on my first night. I relaxed a little and began to enjoy myself. Best of all, I made some good friends. I met a guy named Ted Axelrod at the bar one night; he'd seen me play many times but he was shy and didn't want to press himself forward like some creep, so it was only in this second summer that we became pals. He loved music and had an enormous record collection. He'd play me songs I'd never heard before, and every so often he'd suggest I include them in my live set. One night he came in with a Billie Holiday album and said there was a track on it he'd like to hear me sing. The song was 'I Loves You, Porgy' from *Porgy and Bess*. I learned the song – as a favour to Ted more than anything else – and played it a couple of nights later. Everybody loved my version, especially Ted, so it became a regular number in my set.

53

I hung out with Ted and his friends, Kevin was around some of the time, and playing at the Midtown was cool, so my second summer in Atlantic City was a joy. The thought of going back to teaching kids at the end of it was unbearable, and I decided to see if I could get nightclub work in Philadelphia. I went to the agent who had got me the Midtown job; he knew I'd done well there and offered me a date in a supper club, the Pooquesin, which was a private bar and considerably more upmarket. I played the same set and it went down as well as ever.

While I was there I met another agent who offered me more work around town. For the usual cut he got me work at places like the High-Thigh, a typical supper club – chic decor, bad food, tasteful singer, expensive drinks, the kind of place a man liked to take a woman to. These clubs were an improvement on the Midtown because they paid more, but the audiences were much less rewarding. Sometimes I was regarded as part of the general ambience and people would try to talk while I played. When that happened I'd give them the old Midtown stare with both barrels, and although none of my students were around to back me up it usually worked. The club customers were a lot wealthier than the Midtown crowd and less shy about asking for requests. I didn't mind that, because if you played it they always tipped, and there's no tipper more extravagant than a man out to impress his woman.

Now that I was appearing in Philadelphia the old problem with Momma raised its head. Eventually she would find out what I was doing and I certainly wasn't going to lie to her about it if she asked, so I broke the news. I told her the reason I played nightclubs was to raise money to finish my education and be the first black classical concert pianist; I told her I never drank liquor when I went to these places, and I told her I played a mixture of classical music and spirituals. It made no difference. I was out in 'the world', as she called it, and there was no forgiving that unless I repented. Once I'd told her, Momma never mentioned it again; she wanted no part of any success I might have because it was sinful and profane, and she would never be able to be proud of me.

Momma's attitude hurt, but I wasn't surprised. It was strange how guilty she made me feel for working towards what she'd always wanted, but there were some things her beliefs didn't allow her to accept – although that didn't include the money I gave her every

My father, John Divine Waymon

Carrol while he was in the army (ABOVE LEFT)

Lucille, my much-loved sister, who died aged 46 (ABOVE RIGHT)

Eunice Waymon, aged 12 (OPPOSITE)

All music is what
awakes within us when we
are reminded by the instru...
It is not the violins or the clarin...
It is not the score of the baritone singing mea...
Nor the sweet romanza; nor that of the women's chorus—
Nor that of the women's chorus—
It is nearer and farther than they—

Lovingly,
— Eunice Waymon—
Age 12

One of my first publicity shots taken in Atlantic City in 1957 (TOP)

My wedding day on 4 December 1961 with Andy (third from right) and his family
(BOTTOM)

With Andy in 1961 (ABOVE LEFT)

The picture taken for a record cover when I was eight months' pregnant (ABOVE RIGHT)

Leaving the maternity hospital with Andy and Lisa in 1962

Arriving and performing at an all-black concert in Mount Morris Park, New York in 1969 (OPPOSITE, ABOVE)

At a civil rights meeting in 1965. On my right are Lorraine Hansberry and Andrew Young (OPPOSITE, LEFT)

At the piano with Lisa in London in 1967 (Syndication International) (ABOVE)

Paris, 1967

month, money earned out in 'the world'. And although when he was sat next to Momma Daddy looked as if he thought working in nightclubs meant I was lost to the devil, I knew he was thrilled. The night I told Momma he sat in the kitchen nodding his head at the things she said, agreeing with her 100 per cent.

A couple of days later we sat in his car and talked about life on the road. Daddy was thinking back nearly forty years, to the time when he was an entertainer around Pendleton, before he met Momma. He knew what the life was like and tried to tell me how it paid well but took its toll in other ways. To me, playing clubs was only a way of getting to be a concert pianist, so his warnings about the dangers of being a performer, the way he kept saying I would have to keep myself 'clean', seemed more funny than anything else. Daddy knew I was scared by some of the things I saw, but my fear was based on ignorance and I didn't really know anything about a performer's life. He remembered what it was like and tried to give me an idea of what to expect. I listened, but didn't really understand.

As 1956 came around I spent my time playing clubs around Philly, teaching music a little and studying hard under Vladimir Sokhaloff. I was playing most nights, but I was earning enough to take extra classes and had more time to practise. Summer arrived, and Harry and his cigar were waiting for me at the Midtown. Kevin wasn't working Atlantic City that year but Ted was there, with a new group of friends all waiting to meet me and hear me play. That was nice, but somehow the Midtown and Atlantic City were nowhere near as much fun as I remembered. The novelty of playing to an audience was long gone, and the place seemed tacky after the Philadelphia supper clubs.

I was lonely. Kevin had been a good friend, and I never knew how good until she was gone. I liked Ted a lot and he was a friend too, but in many ways he was simply a kind and sensitive fan. I wanted someone to be close to, somebody around me who would be there all the time, not just when I played.

One night at the bar I got talking to a white boy, a good-looking man with a slow smile and charm. He came on to me in a sweet way and made me laugh. The next night he was there again, waiting at the bar with my glass of milk in his hand. His name was Don Ross.

He dressed scruffy because he thought of himself as a beatnik and that was their style. He looked a little like a young Dustin Hoffman.

If you asked him what he did he'd say he was a painter or a drummer – depending on what kind of mood he was in – but in fact he was a pitchman and travelled up and down the East Coast working the fairs. He'd mark his pitch, set up his stall and sell whatever it was that day by shouting out as people walked by. He sold anything: toys, orchids, food, whatever. Pitching got him enough money to get by and when he earned enough to live he stopped and hung out with his beat crowd. They'd find someone with a big house and move in, lazing around, drinking some, smoking a little hash, listening to records, getting off on the beat writers. The whole hipster thing.

Don had heard about me from his friends and come down to the Midtown to hear me play. Pretty soon he became a regular and we'd chat at the bar in between my sets. He started to walk me home at night and then came round to see me during the day as well, taking me out and introducing me to the crowd he mixed with. Very quickly I grew to rely on him being around, and if he missed a night at the Midtown the place felt empty and I got lonely again. After a while we slid into bed together, and if I didn't feel a great deal of passion for him it was nice to wake up in his arms rather than on my own in a cold room. Don eased into my life in the same way, never setting me on fire but taking the edge off my isolation and surrounding me with an affection I needed. It was a kind of loving you can get used to very quickly and before I knew it the idea of being without him was unthinkable. He loved me, and I needed to be loved.

I was starting to get offers of work from clubs outside Atlantic City and Philadelphia, and Don wanted me to take them up. He was used to travelling all over and promised to come with me when he could, but I was nervous, not trusting the promises I got made. What I needed was someone to come in and take charge of my career – a manager; but I still didn't think of my club work as a career at all – it was simply a way to raise the money to go back to Juilliard. One evening in the Midtown Harry introduced me to a friend of his who – he said – had heard about me in New York and come down to see what all the fuss was about. I found out later this was horse feathers. Jerry Fields – this was the friend – had been in Atlantic City anyhow and had stopped by the previous night to catch my show, which he liked. He'd never met Harry before either.

Jerry was an agent who worked out of New York. All the agents I'd worked with up to then – the guy who got me the Midtown job and the guy in Philly – were small-time bookers working out of their home towns. Jerry was a proper New York agent who had a good reputation in the business and a roster of artists that he worked hard to develop by placing them in the right venues at the right moment.

All of this I would find out later. What happened in the Midtown was that Jerry promised me work in New York that would pay more than anything I was being offered, said he wanted to be my exclusive agent, added that he thought it very likely I could get a recording session, and said if we shook hands there and then that would do for him until the contracts were drawn up and signed. I asked him to let me think about it. He said, 'I'm offering you more money so what's to think about?' I thought about that for a few seconds and then stretched out my hand across the table. Jerry Fields was my agent from that moment until the day he died, which was about five years later.

Before he left for New York Jerry said he'd let me know about dates as soon as he had any news. In the meantime I was committed to playing some club dates in Philly, and I got ready to leave the Midtown for the last time. Don went pitching upcoast but promised to come as soon as he could; he arrived in Philly a couple of weeks later.

Nobody at home was at all bothered about me going with Don: the Waymon family wasn't prejudiced, so his colour was never an issue, and he got on fine with everybody. Momma was the only person who might have made a fuss, and that would have been because of what Don did for a living rather than anything else; but she saw him as part of the sinful world I had fallen into, and I already knew what she thought about that. I went ahead with the club dates, which were just the same as ever except for the fact that one night, without my knowing it, somebody recorded one of my sets. That night I sang 'I Loves You, Porgy', 'Since My Lover Has Gone', 'Black is the Colour', 'Lovin' Woman' and 'Baubles, Bangles and Beads', and the recording appeared years later as a pirate album called *Starring Nina Simone*. I had to take the record label to court in 1965 to stop them selling it. So the first album I ever made was a pirate that I never got paid for and knew nothing about. It was an omen for how record companies were going to treat me.

Jerry called from New York. He'd arranged a string of gigs for me in supper clubs on the East Side, as well as others in upstate New York and in Pennsylvania after Christmas. One of the dates was at a club next to a theatre in a place called New Hope – the New Hope Playhouse Inn. It was nowhere special. After my first show there I got talking with some people who had just come from seeing a jazz trio at another club nearby. The guitarist in the trio was a friend of theirs and they suggested it might be fun if he and I played together.

People do this to artists all the time, suggesting that they jam with some complete stranger when the poor sucker is working hard enough just trying to keep it going to the end of the week. I wasn't impressed by the idea at all. I knew jazz musicians who liked to get up and blow with whoever was around, but I wasn't a jazz musician and I didn't see why I should be expected to play with a man I had never met before. I was discouraging about the whole thing, but the next night before my second set started this gawky Jewish kid walked in. He was thinner than a skinned snake and carried his guitar in one hand and his amp in the other. He came over and introduced himself, said his name was Al Schackman and he'd heard some good things about me. I'd certainly never heard of Al Schackman and I eyed him with suspicion. But he'd driven over to play and I didn't want to seem rude, so I sat down at the piano and waited for him to set up. When he was finally ready he looked over and I called the title of the first song, 'Little Girl Blue'.

What happened next was one of the most amazing moments in my entire life. Remember that I wasn't anything like a typical nightclub pianist: I wasn't a jazz player but a classical musician, and I improvised arrangements of popular songs using classical motifs. It's not a predictable art. For example, before I started playing I wouldn't be able to say where I would come in with the lyric because the number of bars I'd play before starting to sing depended on what I did with the opening section. Although jazz musicians are used to improvising they need to be familiar with how another musician plays before they can really get something going; they have to listen and get their minds on the same track or they get a lot of hesitations and false starts. But when I started in on 'Little Girl Blue' Al was right there with me from the first moment, as if we had been playing together all our lives. It was more than that even: it was as if we were one instrument split it in two – I, the piano, Al, the guitar. I had never felt so much freedom in playing, knowing that someone knew where I was going and I knew where he was going. It was like telepathy – we couldn't lose each other. And Al had perfect pitch, too, so I never had to tell him what key to play.

We played Bach-type fugues and inventions for hours, and all the way through we hardly dared look at each other for fear that the whole thing would come tumbling down and we wouldn't be able to pick it up again.

When we finished that night we talked about playing again sometime soon, and about maybe working together in New York. Al liked the idea – how could he not – so I said maybe he'd like to come down to Philadelphia the next weekend to rehearse a little. We both knew that we weren't going to rehearse anything the next weekend – we were just going to get up and play and go wherever the music took us. Calling it a rehearsal was just a way of making something so deliciously wonderful sound like hard work. At the Midtown I'd discovered the joy of creating my own music, and now here in a small town I'd discovered the joy of sharing it. No wonder the place was called New Hope.

We 'rehearsed' together whenever we could through the first part of 1957, but Al was working a lot with Burt Bacharach at the time and had to go out to the West Coast for a while. I missed him, and not just his playing, because we became friends very quickly and found that we had the same type of understanding between us when we weren't playing, as if we were twins. Sometimes we'd be talking on the phone to each other and we'd say exactly the same word at exactly the same time. Weird.

That week in New Hope was certainly touched by something, because Jerry called to say that a demo tape I had made at the Inn before Al came down to play had been heard by some guys from a label called Bethlehem Records in New York, and they wanted to talk to me about recording an album. The next day Sid Nathan, the owner of Bethlehem, turned up at my house. He had a bunch of songs with him he expected me to play and a list of musicians he wanted me to use as my studio band. I knew Jerry hadn't warned Sid about me, because he started gulping like a fish when I told him I wasn't interested in playing any of his songs and that if I was going to make an album I'd choose the material myself and pick the musicians I wanted to support me.

What Sid Nathan didn't know was I wasn't interested in being famous, and I didn't think being a singer was any big thing. All the time I was playing those little tours up and down the East Coast I made sure that I got back to Philadelphia every week for my lesson with Vladimir Sokhaloff. I never missed one, and I never stopped preparing my pieces for the next week's lesson. Clubs weren't my serious ambition, so if the money wasn't right and it wasn't fun I wouldn't play.

It was difficult for a man like Sid Nathan to understand that an unknown girl who made a living playing small clubs could turn down a record deal without thinking twice about it. He came back to the house later in the afternoon and said I could do whatever I wanted so long as I left with him the next day to go to the studio. I spoke to Jerry and he said the money they were offering was fine, so I agreed.

I went into the studio and recorded my songs exactly as I always played them, so when you listen to that Bethlehem album you're hearing the songs played as they were at the Midtown Bar. The only difference is that you don't get to hear the improvisations that I wove around those numbers in my live set. 'I Loves You, Porgy' was the song I sang for Ted; 'For All We Know' was my usual closing number; 'You'll Never Walk Alone' and 'He's Got the Whole World in His Hands' I'd sung all my life; and 'Plain Gold Ring' was a song I learned from the harpist Kitty White. I made up the arrangement of 'Little Girl Blue' and 'Good King Wenceslas' one night at the Midtown. I learned 'He Needs Me' from Peggy Lee. 'African Mailman' was made up on the spot in the studio and recorded in one take. 'Central Park Blues' was the same; I called it that because we'd just been out into Central Park to shoot publicity photos for the album cover.

We recorded the whole session in fourteen hours and the last song we did was 'My Baby Just Cares For Me', which I included because Sid wanted an up-tempo number to finish. I was back home in Philadelphia two days after I left, and I spent the next three days playing Beethoven to get the recording session out of my system. My biggest regret was that Al was still away with Burt Bacharach and couldn't make it to the session.

At the end of the recording Sid gave me a piece of paper to sign, which I did without reading it. It was a standard recording contract. I had no manager, no lawyer and no accountant. What would I need them for? I was a classical pianist, not some pop star. It was a mistake that, in the end, would cost me over a million dollars.

Chapter 5

In New York word got out that I had recorded an album, and even before it was released Jerry started getting more enquiries from clubs looking to book me, mainly supper clubs on the East Side. I played as many as I could get, figuring it was only a matter of time before the balloon would burst, the clubs dry up and all my savings would go on the lessons with Vladimir Sokhaloff. My hope was that maybe I could establish myself in the New York clubs and enrol at Juilliard again. Just in case that didn't happen I carried on at the clubs in Philly, too, keeping myself available.

Bethlehem released the album, *Little Girl Blue*, midway through 1958. I had this idea that when it came out everything would change – I'd make a fortune and be able to give up performing altogether. Nothing's ever that easy. A few music papers picked up on the LP and said good things about it, but when I called Sid Nathan at Bethlehem to ask how it was doing, and should we think about doing shows to promote it, he wouldn't talk to me. I couldn't understand why a company would go to the trouble of making a record and then do nothing about selling it. What sort of sense did that make?

The only person really interested in my record was a white DJ named Sid Marx at a Philadelphia R & B radio station. I knew him from the Philly clubs; he used to come down to see me sometimes and we'd talk a little. Not great friends or anything – we just used to say hello. Sid got hold of a copy of *Little Girl Blue* and started playing it on air. He liked the album a lot, and the track he favoured most was 'I Loves You, Porgy'. Maybe he decided to make the track a hit, because he played it over and over, night and day. He'd play it three or four times in a row sometimes. After a while he didn't have to keep pushing it because people started calling up the station asking for it by name, so the other DJs had to play it too. As soon as that happened

Sid Marx said to me, 'Nina, you've got to get Bethlehem to release "Porgy", it'll hit!'

I called Sid Nathan to let him know what was happening down in Philadelphia, but before I could tell him everybody was asking where they could buy 'Porgy' as a single, he hung up on me. When I tried to call him again no one would put me through. I was confused: the boss of my record company was turning down the chance to make some money. I told Sid and he just shook his head and laughed, like he wasn't surprised. I don't know whether he or some record store owners then called Bethlehem to ask when they were releasing 'Porgy' but some time later they finally did put it out as a single. 'He Needs Me' was the flip side. It hit in Philadelphia instantly, got picked up by the New York stations and within a few weeks had hit all through the eastern seaboard: New York, Philly, down in the South, everywhere.

Altogether it took about six months from the release of my album to 'Porgy' hitting. Jerry Fields was going crazy, and said when I was in New York I must come by his office because we had to talk. I dropped in the next time I was in the city to hear what he had to say, which was very simple: I had a hit and I needed to keep attention on me, so I should work out of New York and leave Philly behind. I needed to be where the action was, in the Big City.

I went home and mentioned it to Don. We'd been together all through this time and, apart from Al Schackman, who wasn't always around, Don was the only person I had to talk to. It wasn't any use talking to Momma because she would have nothing to do with anything connected to show business, and Daddy would only say I should stay in Philadelphia, whatever happened, just so he could be near me.

I got scared thinking about moving to New York. I recalled the last time I'd lived there, in Harlem, and remembered how lonely I'd been. I remembered those guys drinking and fighting on the streets. Even though I had been to New York many times I'd never enjoyed the place and left as quickly as I could. When I was forced to stop there a while I stayed at my Aunt Margaret's house, which reminded me of Tryon and Momma, even though it was in the middle of Harlem.

Something else scared me too: I had found it difficult to make friends in Philadelphia and spent a lot of my time on my own so how would I endure New York, where everybody was rude and cold, unlike the southern people I had grown up with? I knew I had to move – I decided I must – but only if I was sure I wouldn't ever be left on my own, that Don would be with me. Unfortunately there was only one way of making sure of that, which was to do what he'd been asking me to do for the past year – marry him.

So I married Don at the County Clerk's office in Philadelphia towards the end of 1958. I can't remember the exact date and I have nothing from our time together to give me any clue: a good indication of my true feelings towards him. None of my family came – I didn't tell them what I was doing – and the only person there apart from the guy who married us was an employee of the Clerk's office who was passing by and acted as witness. We left for New York right away and spent our 'honeymoon' settling into a tiny room in the house of a woman friend of Ted Axelrod's, the man who had first introduced me to 'Porgy'. Her house was in Greenwich Village and we stayed about a month until we found our own place to rent.

I realized marrying Don was a mistake before that first month ended. I was working as much as I could, trying to save money and at the same time going back to Philadelphia once a week for my lesson. Don meanwhile did nothing except hang out with his friends drinking, smoking and talking poetry, jazz and all the usual beat bullshit. He kept his drum kit and brushes in our room and sat around trying to play or paint while I cleaned up around him, cooked the food, tried to sleep and went out to work in the evenings. And he spent my money when he had none of his own.

Those weeks in New York were miserable. I had a hit record and guaranteed bookings, but no manager to organize my appearances or accountant to advise me. Jerry just handled booking arrangements, nothing else. With the rent to pay and Don to feed, as well as sending money back home to Momma and paying for my piano tuition, there were weeks when I barely came out even. I hit one patch when I was so tired from performing that I asked Jerry to hold off bookings for a while, and then found a week into my rest that my money wouldn't hold out until my next date, ten days away. To fill the gap I took a job as a maid for a white family. I didn't have to think at all – just clean up, fold sheets and wash dishes. It was like a holiday after the tension and unnatural hours of nightclub life: if it had paid more I would have stuck at it.

New Year 1959 found me in a creepy marriage stuck in a tiny room with a hit record, a rising reputation, and no idea how to make the money I needed to finish my classical training. I began to get depressed, edged on by bad habits picked up from my 'husband'. Don was no drunk, but he liked to have stuff around the place and for the first time in my life I drank liquor. It wasn't as good for me as it was for him, because Don drank when he was relaxed and I drank in order to try and relax – there was a difference. At clubs I started to take a glass of champagne after a show: having never drunk before, one glass was enough to set me spinning, and the guys buying would fill my glass when I wasn't looking and one would turn into two and then three and before I knew it I'd be drunk, frightened and rushing to make it home before I got sick. When I got in Don would either be out with his friends or sitting on the floor smoking a reefer, stoned again.

I had originally married Don so I'd never be alone, but after we had got married I went home hoping he wouldn't be there. Some stupid arrangement. I missed my family, but I couldn't go home – not when I'd gone away with hardly a word, off to New York to be a star. I could picture Momma's face, with that I-told-you-so smile, and Daddy standing behind her, happy to have his little baby home and I was twenty-five years old, for God's sake.

Going back to Philadelphia was not an option, so I walked out on Don, packed my things and moved into a little apartment. Don stood and watched but didn't say anything to stop me; he knew we were going nowhere. With him off my back I started practising again, and relaxed with Bach. There was no need to drink any more so I stopped, except for a glass of champagne after the show – and I made sure it was only one glass. And while I was scared I'd be lonely again it didn't turn out that way. Jerry Fields introduced me to a lawyer, Max Cohen, who started to deal with my legal affairs. Max understood my classical background, admired my piano technique and encouraged me to continue studying. He became my first great friend in New York.

I found that during those first two months in the city, when it had seemed the loneliest place in the world, a great deal had happened that I was unaware of: Joyce Selznick, cousin to the film producer David O., was the eastern talent scout for Columbia Pictures Records – Colpix. She knew me from 'Porgy' and the Bethlehem album and had seen my first few dates after I moved to New York, at the very time I was so miserable.

She wanted to sign me to her label. My agreement with Bethlehem was for only one album, so Colpix moved in and offered me a long-term deal. Max Cohen negotiated it for me and we signed the contract in April.

My first album for Colpix was *The Amazing Nina Simone*, but before it even came out Bethlehem had released a rival, *Nina Simone and Her Friends*, which contained the few remaining songs that we had decided not to use on *Little Girl Blue*. I had no idea that Bethlehem had any intention to do such a thing until I saw it on display in a record store window in Greenwich Village, but there was nothing I could do about it. When I signed that slip of paper at the end of the Bethlehem session I gave up all of my rights as a performer and artist, so they could sell recordings of mine that I had never thought of releasing. I would get wise to contracts over the years, but what hurt most was that Bethlehem would not even have had a hit record if I hadn't kept calling them, trying to get them to do the job they said they were so good at. It was thanks to *me* that they were in a position to make money out of my name.

The further I got into the business side of the music industry, the less I liked it. Record companies were bad enough, but it was only a matter of luck that clubs were not a problem for me; I did my shows, got my money and left. I was fortunate not to have trouble from club owners but I always drew a crowd so it made no sense to rip me off – if that happened I'd never play a particular club again. Unlike most artists I didn't care that much about a career as a popular singer. I was different – I was going to be a classical musician. Even after 'Porgy' hit, even after I signed to Colpix, it was all to raise money for proper tuition. So I played what I wanted and nothing else. Hell, they weren't paying me enough to tell me what to play. There was no proper producer on my records – just an engineer to set everything up, an orchestrator to write out the arrangements, and the rest I did myself. If someone had walked up to me in the street and given me $100,000 I would have given up popular music and enrolled at Juilliard and never played in a club again. And I wouldn't have missed the life because I hated it anyway; the cheap crooks, the disrespectful audiences, the way most people were so easily satisfied by dumb, stupid tunes.

But no one offered the money so I kept on working. In the summer I took on my first real manager, Bertha Case. She was a woman I met in New Hope, the same place where I met Al. In normal life she was a literary agent and had come to see a play at the theatre; then she wandered into the club downstairs, heard me, and offered to be my manager. At that time I was working around Philly and Bertha was based in Manhattan so I turned her down. When we met again in New York she repeated the offer and I made the same mistake I had made with Don – I said yes because I wanted someone around. She wasn't used to the music business, and got tired of managing me around the same time I got tired of her. All the important decisions were being taken by Jerry Fields, anyway, who decided the time had come to move out of clubs into larger halls and put me on the bill for a concert at New York City Town Hall on 12 September.

The day of the show I dressed in a long white gown draped over one shoulder and white satin shoes. Don was with me that evening because I was a little nervous – not of performing, but of being around so many people backstage. I needed a familiar face. I stood in the wings and looked out at the audience, sitting in neat rows with no drinks in their hands, no cigarette girls walking up and down to distract them, and no out-of-tune piano to ruin my performance. The MC called my name and I walked on like an Egyptian queen – slow, calm and serious.

All those club dates had been trashy rehearsals for this, the real thing, a concert platform. Miz Mazzy had taught me the way to behave on stage years before, years of practice had developed my musical technique to a point where I had total confidence, and the Midtown Bar had shown me exactly how to deal with an audience. The night belonged to me, as I knew it would from the day Jerry told me he'd booked the hall.

Colpix recorded the concert and released it as *Nina Simone at Town Hall*, so if you don't believe me you can listen for yourself. The reviews were the best I had ever had. I was a sensation. An overnight success, like in the movies.

The New York press went crazy over me, and I found it hard to understand why I was being hailed as a new star. I already had a hit record, I wasn't unknown, so why all the excitement? The reaction of the crowd that night was something else, too. I'd played clubs for years, and although people liked me they had never gone as wild as that before. I had played my usual set, so what was new? The truth came home over the next couple of weeks: it was my audience that had changed – I'd found my Midtown audience again here in New York. These were the same sort of kids, mixed in with the hip New

York jazz crowd and the people who hung out in the Village coffee bars and clubs. Thrown in on top were the folk fans and the beat people like Don, and they all hit on my music.

Suddenly I was the hot new thing, Queen of the Village for a while. I started to get recognized on the street, I was offered concerts all across the States, my records were released in Europe, journalists started pestering me for interviews, and TV producers wanted me for their shows. At first I didn't stop to think about it all – I just went with the tide; but over the next few months I talked about why I had suddenly made it with friends, especially Al Schackman, who was back in town.

The audience that was the first to pick up on me in a really big way were the people who hung out in the Village, the artistic and intellectual crowd. In the Village there were a number of different groupings. There was the jazz scene, with guys like John Coltrane, Art Pepper, George Adams and many more just walking about the place looking for fun and a place to play, which would be a club if they had a paying date, or a loft somewhere if they just wanted to blow. Surrounding them, gravitating around the music, were the writers, poets and painters, remarkable men and women who would become my friends. Langston Hughes, Jimmy Baldwin, Leroi Jones – as Amiri Baraka was known then – Lorraine Hansberry, Godfrey Cambridge, Dick Gregory – so many talented and exciting people. On the outside of them were the folks that understood something special was happening, that it was an extraordinary time to be in the Village, and who were just kicking off from being in there at the heart of it. Mixed in with this crowd were the journalists, film makers and record company guys, the people who were going to package up and exploit this scene just as soon as they got a handle on what it actually was.

The Village Gate was the jazz centre. Politics was mixed in with so much of what went on at the Gate that I remember it now as two sides of the same coin, politics and jazz. Comedians like Dick Gregory, Bill Cosby and Woody Allen opened for the players and it was all part of the same thing – the music and the comedy, the jazz and the politics, it all went together. But the jazz crowd were only part of the story because at the Bitter End – just across the street from the Village Gate – you found the folk crowd, who had a different kind of approach to music and an attitude that wasn't cool like the jazz guys, but who were hip all the same. They had their own heroes around the place, people like Joan Baez, Tim Hardin, Peter, Paul and Mary, Odetta, and this very young guy who sang comedy parodies in the intermissions, Bob Dylan.

Not too many people were so slick that they moved between the jazz and folk scenes, but some did, and in amongst those you found the beat poets, weird writers and artistic drunks. Most people at least knew about what was going on in the other scene and they didn't pass judgement on what they were ignorant of. And the whole thing was multi-racial and integrated, although the folkies were mainly white kids. And everybody in and around these scenes liked to think that they were cool, so when I came along playing music that wasn't much like anything they were used to, they were cool to that – they gave my music a chance, and they found they liked it. And they were cool to me, too: in the words of the time they 'dug' me – they gave me respect.

Shot through everyone in the Village was excitement with what was going on and a hunger to be the first one to discover what was coming next. The folk kids were discovering blues players that the jazz people knew so well they regarded them as old history, nothing to do with what was happening; but to the white kids it was somebody else's history they were hearing, so it was new and exciting. And the jazz players had their ears and minds open to other influences – they had to, or else they wouldn't be able to play like they did.

This was the crowd I plugged into when I played Town Hall. I was lucky because life in the Village had given these people the right sort of attitude: if it sounded good, appreciate it for what it was and don't get too uptight if you can't decide what to call it.

After Town Hall critics started to talk about what sort of music I was playing and tried to find a neat slot to file it away in. It was difficult for them because I was playing popular songs in a classical style with a classical piano technique influenced by cocktail jazz. On top of that I included spirituals and children's songs in my perform-ances, and those sorts of songs were automatically identified with the folk movement. So saying what sort of music I played gave the critics problems because there was something from everything in there, but it also meant I was appreciated across the board – by jazz, folk, pop and blues fans as well as admirers of classical music.

They finally ended up describing me as a 'jazz-and-something-else-singer'. To me 'jazz' meant a way of thinking, a way of being, and the black man in America was jazz in everything he did – in the way he walked, talked, thought and acted. Jazz music was just another aspect of the whole thing, so in that sense because I was black I was a jazz singer, but in every other way I most definitely wasn't.

Because of 'Porgy' people often compared me to Billie Holiday, which I hated. That was just one song out of my repertoire, and anybody who saw me perform could see we were entirely different. What made me mad was that it meant people couldn't get past the fact we were both black: if I had happened to be white nobody would have made the connection. And I didn't like to be put in a box with other jazz singers because my musicianship was totally different, and in its own way superior. Calling me a jazz singer was a way of ignoring my musical background because I didn't fit into white ideas of what a black performer should be. It was a racist thing; 'If she's black she must be a jazz singer.' It diminished me, exactly like Langston Hughes was diminished when people called him a 'great black poet'. Langston was a great poet period, and it was up to him and him alone to say what part the colour of his skin had to do with that.

If I had to be called something it should have been a folk singer, because there was more folk and blues than jazz in my playing. Whatever I was, the people in the Village liked it and word spread out across the country. By the end of the year I had played at the Village Vanguard; the Casino Royal, Washington; the Town House, Pittsburgh; the Blue Note, Chicago; and the Hollywood Bowl. I was also having to get used to fame very quickly: just a month after Town Hall I was playing at the Showboat in Philadelphia when I heard that my sister Frances had just given birth to her first baby; it was 16 October 1959. I jumped up at the end of my first show and grabbed a cab to the hospital. The minute I got inside the place it went wild, with all the other visitors running over to me, asking for autographs, touching my hair and my clothes, and pushing me into a corner of the ward in their excitement. Husbands, fathers, grandmothers, aunts and uncles all crowded in around me. Behind them in their beds, alone and forgotten, sat all the young mothers with their new-born babies. They had to put Frances, her baby and me in a private room so I could visit in peace, and the whole time I was in there people stood outside the door with their noses pressed against the glass, just staring.

I was moving fast now – touring constantly, getting ready to record again and being swamped with offers to get involved with all sorts of projects. In the middle of all this I received through the mail a cheque for $10,000 from Bethlehem Records, representing royalties on the two albums they had out. I was rich, or at least no longer poor.

Ten thousand dollars! It would have taken me two and a half years to earn that much working at Arlene's Studio. The first thing I did was send some of it down to Momma, then I moved into an apartment on 103rd Street, on the 12th floor. It was gorgeous, with seven pastel-painted rooms – one of them a huge bathroom – and walk-in wardrobes. It was fully furnished and carpeted throughout. And there was a live-in maid named Mary. Then I went down to the showrooms with Al and bought a steel-grey Mercedes convertible with red leather upholstery and matching luggage. I bought a red hat that matched the rest, put the roof of the Mercedes down and cruised around the Village for hours, looking so fine.

I was determined to enjoy this life for as long as it lasted, and when I had time I'd walk around the Village, stopping off at Rienzi's Coffee House on McDougal for iced coffee and coffee icecream. I made friends with Odetta and I'd see her there and we'd sit and watch the world go by, talk, may be shop, but usually just relax. I took time to go to museums, picture galleries and poetry readings – I saw Ginsberg at a loft reading, didn't like his poems too much but he was sweet – and generally lived the life I'd promised myself, at least I did between touring across country and going back for tuition with Carl Friedberg.

For a while I felt good about myself, sitting in my own apartment with my own car parked outside, taking lessons at Juilliard again, just like I'd always hoped to when I was playing clubs in Philly or singing under the leaky umbrella at the Midtown.

My next ambition as a performer was to get to the point where I would never have to play in a dive again, where I could make more money by playing one concert in a proper hall than I could from taking a residency of a week or two in a club. But if I *had* to play clubs there were worse ones to headline than the Village Gate, which was where I started in 1960.

Colpix recorded my set there and it became my next album, *Live at Village Gate*. Opening the show was a young comedian, Richard Pryor, and on the first night of my booking I stood in the wings with him as he waited to go on. He shook like he had malaria, he was so nervous. I couldn't bear to watch him shiver, so I put my arms around him there in the dark and rocked him like a baby until he calmed down. The next night was the same, and the next, and I rocked him each time. He never stopped being nervous – at least not while I was there.

I was always treated properly at the Gate. Art D'Lugoff was the owner and we got to know each other well. Art treated performers as equals, as people worthy of respect. One of the reasons I hated clubs so much was the way owners made you feel, as if they were doing you a favour letting you play when in fact you were the reason they stayed in business at all. Often, out on the road at some hole in the wall, I would find myself fighting to get paid at three in the morning after travelling hours to get there and playing half the night for the money. At the Village Gate it was different. Art became a friend and invited me over to his house for dinner many times. He understood that respect was important: when it was due he gave it, and got it back in return.

Those first months after Town Hall my life blazed, and for a moment I thought I had everything I wanted. There was money and the promise of more, together with fame and respect. After shows people would crowd my dressing room, leave flowers, kiss me and say they loved me. Men I had never met before, handsome men, said they loved me and I almost believed them – I wanted it to be true. I went to parties with movie stars and died of embarrassment when they came over to talk to me. Rod Steiger walked over one time with Natalie Wood – she was so tiny – and he started talking; but I couldn't speak; I just couldn't make any sound come out of my mouth I was so shy and nervous and ashamed at being such a wreck. Another time I met Lauren Bacall and she knew who I was, she knew my music. Unbelievable.

Worst of all was when I went to see Frank Sinatra in Atlantic City and left before the end because I didn't want to be recognized when the lights went up. I heard later that the woman I had been sitting next to was a friend of Sinatra's and she said to him after the show 'Guess who was here? Nina Simone.' And Sinatra said 'Why didn't anybody tell me? Why wasn't she up here with me?' I cried for a year when I heard that.

Yet all the time I didn't quite believe it. Don and I had agreed to divorce the year before and it came through while I was playing the Gate that spring. I was on my own again: no boyfriend, no manager. I wasn't lonely like I had been in Philadelphia because I had Al

Schackman, Odetta and Max Cohen, all people that I could talk to and go out with; and there were parties to go to, with famous people to stand next to, even if I was usually too shy to say anything. But once I'd done that a few times the glamour wore off and the doubts that were always inside me started to surface again. Some days I found myself sitting down and thinking; 'I'm working hard, I'm earning good money, I'm successful, people respect me, I'm doing well – so why aren't I happy?'

The people I saw, the stars I met, all went past in a blur because I was moving so fast. The bookings started to come in thick and fast and I had no manager to organize my schedule so I accepted dates I should have refused, took too many long-term bookings, ran from club to concert hall to airport, always rushing. I averaged five shows a week for over a year without any kind of organized back-up. I thought it would all end some time and I'd get some rest and have the time to appreciate what I'd done, but it never happened. And I was always tired: if I said that a thousand times it wouldn't be enough. I was always tired.

In the summer I played the Newark Jazz Festival and did my first TV show. I intended to take a break straight after, but Jerry booked me into a club in New York, Basin Street East. I didn't have a good time and thought about quitting the place because they weren't paying me properly. I was so tired of this kind of treatment. In the audience one night I noticed my hairdresser Johnny sitting with Marguerite Mathis, Johny Mathis's sister, and with them was a light-skinned man I hadn't met before. I stopped by during the intermission to say hello and took a look at the stranger. He invited me to sit down with them, so I did. He introduced himself: his name was Andrew Stroud, and he was a bank teller. He didn't say much, just sat watching as Johnny, Maguerite and I talked. He'd ordered some potatoes from the kitchen but hadn't eaten them so as we chatted I picked at them one by one.

The time came for me to go back, and I finished the last of the potatoes just in time. Before I could get up Andrew asked me if I wanted to go out for a drink after the show. I looked at him more carefully. He was just a little taller than me, well built – about 190 pounds I guessed – and neatly dressed. He wore an African medallion around his neck. He seemed very sure of himself, very unflustered. I liked that, so I said, sure, I'd go uptown to Harlem with him after the show. He was waiting for me when I came off, and we caught a cab. I had a good time that night and made another date.

Andrew had lied to me. He wasn't a bank teller at all, but a cop – a detective sergeant in the 26th Precinct, and had been that for fourteen years. A tough man. The 26th Precinct was Harlem, so you just knew he'd seen a few things. People around town said he wasn't the sort of man you messed around with, and Frankie Lymon said he once saw Andrew throw a man off a roof. Frankie was a junkie and you couldn't always believe what he said, but the real point was if somebody told that story about the roof nobody in Harlem laughed. They didn't know if it was true but they could believe it – they could imagine Andy throwing a guy off a roof. He didn't say anything about it either way, but he had a strong and solid air about him, that made you think 'Well, maybe . . .'

Andy wasn't tough to be around, not domineering, but you knew all the time he was there. Sitting in my dressing room with my back to the door I knew the moment Andy came in even if I couldn't see him, because I felt his personality around me. On our first dates I realized his reputation when we went into a club or a bar. First of all everybody knew him and he knew everybody. Some guys would look up as he came into the room, check him, and just slide away without saying hello. The people that he did talk to were always very respectful and quiet, because Andy hated a guy getting too excited in his ear. Andy was quiet and calm always, and always in control. That's what I liked most about him, that I felt safe when he was around. No one would dare to do anything to me with Andy there.

He carried a gun, and although I never saw him use it I knew it was there under his arm as we chatted or danced. He had told me he was a bank teller when we first met because he thought I might be put off by the fact he was a cop. He didn't tell me the truth until late into our second date. I knew I liked him by then anyway, and when he told me I just squealed and liked him more. He dealt with murders, drugs, protection rackets, the whole lot – a world that I knew nothing about but which seemed so exciting, especially the fact that he wouldn't talk about it much, only occasionally saying something which conjured up a dark world of gangsters and vice men, Edward G. Robinson and Humphrey Bogart shooting it out down a back alley late at night.

I suppose dating a singer, a star of concert halls and nightclubs, had some of the same effect for Andy, although his imagination wasn't as innocent as mine. I knew he was serious about me from that first night in Harlem but I took things easy, let him do the chasing and settled back to enjoy it. He walked me back up to the front door of my apartment on our second or third date and wanted to come in, but I pecked him on the cheek and shut the door. I heard him laughing in the hallway and then his keys jangled and he said, 'I'm a cop, haven't you ever heard of skeleton keys?' He played around with the lock for a few seconds and then swung the door open, looked at me standing with my mouth open wide enough to catch flies, said 'Goodnight' and closed it again.

He sent me flowers all the time and gave me jewels – diamonds. I never asked how he could afford them on a cop's salary. Andy had been married three times before, so he knew women and he knew how to be around them, how they like to be treated. He understood that I was shy and set about bringing me out of myself slowly, without rushing too fast. I opened up to him. All my time in New York, even though I was successful I could never relax enough to enjoy myself; performing, dealing with agents and managers, doing interviews, they all pulled me tighter and tighter, like an overwound watch. Andy came along and time slowed down when we were together and I could wind down: he relaxed me like a good massage.

I needed someone like him waiting offstage after some of my shows. We dated through the winter of 1960 and in February 1961 I played the Apollo, Harlem. Friends said I might have trouble with the crowd there because the Apollo was well known for giving artists a rough time and I was well known for doing the same to audiences. So the two of us getting together was looked at as a kind of championship boxing match, with the Apollo as the champ and me the contender. In the end we fought to a draw. I found out how rude the place could be when I started to introduce a song and people laughed at me. I didn't know what for, whether it was because of my southern accent or the way I presented myself – with dignity and style instead of looking like a Christmas decoration, which was what they were used to – but anyhow I stopped playing and gave them a quick talk about manners.

The Apollo went quiet and I started into the song – 'Worksong', a tune written around an old chain gang chant – and as I played I saw three Harlem ladies walking straight down the aisle towards the stage. I guessed they were ladies because they wore dresses, but that was really the only clue they gave; underneath their hats and corsets they moved like all-in wrestlers. I kept playing, but my mind wandered to thinking about the distance from my piano stool to the side of the stage. They stopped at the footlights, dipped their hands into their purses and scattered a shower of coins on the floor around my feet. Then they stuck their noses in the air, turned on their heels and stalked out. Once they'd gone the atmosphere loosened and the rest of the show went fine – in fact for a moment I thought I might have been enjoying myself. I never played the Apollo again, though, and I was asked many times.

I went back to the Village Gate in April and enjoyed it once more. Andy was in the crowd most nights and we spent the days together. Between shows I rehearsed for a Broadway revue I'd agreed to appear in. Brendan Behan – who was already more famous for his drinking than his writing – was the MC and I was to perform two songs in the middle of the show. Rather than doing a show on my own, taking all the responsibility myself, I was sharing it with a group of performers and I liked that. Backstage was full of people laughing and talking, having affairs, being jealous of each other – the whole Broadway thing. I'd never been in a show where I had to take directions about my performance, either. I didn't mind at all; it was less effort than having to think about it myself. Brendan always came in drunk, but it didn't stop him concentrating.

I interrupted rehearsals to go down to Philadelphia for a concert on 3 July. I hadn't been feeling too good for a couple of days and thought I was getting a cold, so I dosed myself with aspirin and throat lozenges to make the trip. By the time I got to Philly I felt really bad. I made it to my dressing room, fainted, and woke up in hospital a couple of days later drugged to the skies and not knowing where I was. I looked over to one side and saw Andy sitting there with a surgical mask over his mouth: that was when I got scared. The doctors came in and turned me over to do a spinal tap. It hurt like hell and I fainted again. I came round later and Andy was still there, still in his mask, holding my hand.

The doctors said I had either non-paralytic polio or spinal mening-itis, they didn't know which. When I heard the word 'meningitis' I started to cry, remembering my brother Harold and what that disease had done to him. I slipped in and out of sleep, and each time I woke I petrified myself with thoughts of paralysis, wheelchairs and the end of not only my show-business career but of any piano playing at all. And the whole time I lay there part of me was saying, 'I told you. I told you it wouldn't last. I told you you'd be punished.'

All I had to hold on to was Andy's hand. He was working every day but he came down to Philly each night, stayed with me until dawn and then drove back to work in Harlem in the morning. They gave me another spinal tap, more drugs, and after about nine days I started improving. The day came when my head cleared, I knew where I was and what was going on, and I knew I was going to get better. Andy had been waiting for that day. He stood up over the bed – still wearing his mask – and said, 'When you get better, once you get out of here, we're going to get married.' I laughed and cried at the same time, and I nodded my head: I loved this man, and needed him too – I knew that now.

I was released from hospital after seventeen days and recovered slowly back home in New York. It was two months before I worked again. In the meantime I took Andy to meet my family. They all got on fine – there wasn't much choice because it was obvious I was determined to marry him – and Momma liked Andy a whole lot, was totally charmed by him. Daddy was different; although he didn't say anything I knew he wasn't happy about Andy, and when we got alone together I asked him about it. Daddy was worried that Andy had been married three times before and asked me if I was entirely sure I wanted to do it. I said yes. He kind of looked away and said if I was sure then go ahead, he wouldn't say anything more about it. But I could tell he was worried, and had reservations.

Andy and I went back to New York and a short while later decided to go out one evening to celebrate our engagement, which we hadn't been able to do before because of my sickness. We went dancing in Harlem, at a small club. Andy was always a quiet man, never spoke too much, but once we got to the club he was taciturn, hardly saying anything. He never drank much either, but that night he started drinking rum, white Puerto Rican rum, and the more he drank the quieter he got. Late in the evening I was walking across the dance floor when a fan stopped me, wanting me to sign something, and when I'd given this guy my autograph he gave me a note, which I slipped into my pocket. This sort of thing happened to me all the time. Andy had seen the guy give me the note, and when I got back to our table he asked me what it was. I told him. He didn't believe me. I laughed – I couldn't believe he'd get jealous on the night we went out to celebrate our engagement.

Andy got up and walked out so I followed him on to the street and found him looking for a cab. When I walked up to him he turned around and hit me. Then he turned back to find his cab, then he hit me again. A cab came and he pushed me in it, got in himself and gave the driver my address. He hit me in the cab, on the pavement outside my apartment building, in the lobby of the building, in the elevator up to the twelfth floor and along the passageway to my apartment.

When we got inside the apartment I was already bleeding. Andy walked around like a madman, shouting and turning over furniture. I was trying to tell him that there was nothing to be jealous of, but he wasn't listening. Months before I'd told him that I'd kept Edney's love letters, the ones he'd written to me when I was at school in Asheville. Andy took out his gun, pointed it at my head and told me to fetch those letters.

I ran to find them, and when I came back into the room with the little bundle done up with a ribbon he took them from me, tied my hands behind my back and sat me on a chair. He put his gun down and started going through Edney's letters, making me read bits out, asking me about them, and if he wasn't satisfied with the answer he hit me again. And again.

He'd lost his mind. It went on like that for hours, with Andy accusing me of having affairs with all sorts of people, throwing Edney's letters in my face, hitting me, screaming. I sat tied up like his prisoner, bleeding and shaking, scared out of my skin. After five hours he stood me up, kicked over the chair and took me into my bedroom. He tied me to the bed and forced himself on me. Afterwards he fell asleep and I twisted out of the cord around my hands and ran out.

I hid out at a friend's house for two weeks, not showing my face to anyone. I heard that Andy was looking for me, but I didn't call or make any effort to let him know where I was. Finally I started going out again, and as soon as it was known I had been seen in the Village Andy found me, sitting in a coffee bar. My eyes were still half-closed and bruised from the beating. Andy looked at me and said, 'Who beat you up like that?' When I said, 'You did,' he denied it absolutely. I looked at him and realized he had no idea what he'd done. He just stared at me. I looked at him and said, 'You're insane.'

He couldn't believe he'd done it. He went to two psychiatrists to see what they said about him; I made him go because he refused to accept that anything had changed between us and acted as if that terrible night just didn't exist. He wanted us to get married like we'd planned, as if nothing had happened. Eventually, with the help of analysis, he did come to accept he had done what I said he had, but he swore it was a freak accident caused by the rum. The psychiatrists came back with different opinions. One said straight out I shouldn't marry him; the other that Andy had been temporarily insane but it probably wouldn't happen again and whether or not we got married was up to me – he wouldn't say either way. Andy begged me to believe it wouldn't happen again.

It was an impossible decision to make. All the reasons for marrying Andy were still there: when he was around I didn't feel lonely, and I could imagine living with him for years and years; the idea was comforting. He said he wanted children and I wanted children too, I wanted a family, wanted to be a wife and mother instead of a performing machine. He said we would buy a house with a garden and a nursery for the baby and I could spend the first six months of our marriage planning how the house would be decorated, choosing furnishings, living a family life. After years of being on my own travelling to clubs and halls all over America I can't describe how wonderful the idea of domestic life seemed to me at that moment. If I turned him down I would be walking away from a security I hadn't felt since I was little girl, since before Daddy got sick.

The way I looked at it, if I married Andy he would be able to protect me from everything but himself. As time passed, and Andy was as attentive and loving as he had been while I was in hospital, the feelings of dread and terror that I had felt when I was around him began to change. The memory of that brutal night didn't fade, but it was opposed by the knowledge of what I would lose if I turned Andy away. If Andy were to go out of my life I would have nobody again, no one to share my success with, no one to go home to, no one to tell me funny stories and hold me in his arms late at night when I couldn't sleep. In the end my loneliness and insecurity made my mind up for me. Andy was a strong man and I loved him. I forced myself to believe he wouldn't hit me any more.

We were married on 4 December 1961, in my apartment on 103rd

Street. I dressed all in white – a white suit and veil, white shoes, fifteen white roses in my arms. His five brothers, my sister Frances, the two psychiatrists, Al Schackman and Ted Axelrod attended. Daddy didn't come.

Chapter 6

I hadn't been married to Andy for more than a few days before I had to leave him and America behind and fly to Lagos in Nigeria. I went as one of a party of thirty or so Afro-American artists and intellectuals under the banner of AMSAC, the American Society of African Culture. They were opening a new cultural centre in Lagos and hosting an inaugural conference and concert series to celebrate the event. I knew about AMSAC because of my friendship with Langston Hughes and Jimmy Baldwin: they took me along to a couple of meetings, and Langston helped to get me on the party. Langston had been the great poet-hero of Harlem for as long as anyone could remember, and Jimmy, who had set the Village alight with *The Fire Next Time*, was a wonderful, mischievous child-genius at Langston's side, with his great round eyes which for some reason always made him look slightly sad. That word 'party' was the right one because, although there were plenty of fanciful speeches and high-minded aims to the trip, I didn't think about any of them. I was just excited about going to Africa.

We flew to Europe on 20 December and connected with a flight to Lagos. I looked out over miles and miles of jungle as we flew until we dropped down to land and the blunt heat of Africa hit us. Outside on the tarmac I could hear the drums going and the songs of welcome starting up. When I got to the door I saw crowds stretched out all round, musicians and dancers, local politicians in their traditional African clothes in a small group at the bottom of the steps, schoolchildren waving and running through the crowd. We stood, all of us, blinking in the sun at the celebrations our arrival had triggered. All around us were black faces, and I felt for the first time the spiritual relaxation any Afro-American feels on reaching Africa. I didn't feel like I'd come home when I arrived in Lagos, but I knew I'd arrived somewhere important and that Africa mattered to me, and would always matter. The people of Lagos never made me feel anything other than welcome but it wasn't Nigeria I arrived in – it was *Africa*.

After a few days, all too quickly over, we returned home. Al Schackman and a couple of other musicians had made the trip with me, but Andy had stayed home and wanted me back as quickly as possible. Leaving Africa after such a short introduction was cruel, but my new husband wanted me in New York and all I could do was promise myself that one day I would return.

Back home Andy and I moved into a house at 406 Nuber Avenue in Mount Vernon, a New York suburb. Our house was big and old with lots of rooms, and set in four acres of land. There were trees everywhere, like Tryon. We had very different taste in furnishings and our first arguments as a married couple were about whether the house should be fitted out with modern stuff (Andy's taste) or antiques (mine).

I realized very quickly that, although the circumstances of my life had changed the reality was still the same: I had to work all the time. At the house we had a Jamaican maid who had to be told what to do every day, and when I wasn't looking over her shoulder I was keeping an eye open outside for the gardener, telling him what I wanted. I found running a household not much less exhausting than doing all the work myself, but Andy wanted things that way – and, to be truthful, so did I. At the Village Gate or in a recording studio somewhere I had often dreamt about a domestic life – it seemed like bliss – but in the flesh it just wore me out. On top of my wifely duties there were some part-time motherly ones because Andy had three kids from his earlier marriages, so when they were around I became a stepmother, too.

The kids visited on weekends and on Saturday mornings we'd all go swimming together, or bicycling. Andy bought a tandem for the two of us and little bikes for the kids and we'd ride out around Mount Vernon, in and out of the trees. On weekdays at home there were more solitary pleasures; I still had my Mercedes, and it gave me more of a thrill than my father's old Ford ever had. Daddy came up to visit soon after I was married – he visited me more often than Momma, who was busy in the church and still didn't approve of my career – and we crept out together just as we used to, except this time it was the Mercedes we stole away in. I let Daddy drive – a real concession because nobody, but nobody, was allowed to drive it except me – and he didn't say much, just sucked his teeth as he felt the power of the car, smiled and started to whistle. Out of the two of us I don't know who was prouder at that moment.

Andy resigned from the Police Department to become my full-time manager, and he was the best manager I ever had, without question. The music business is full of thieves, so it makes sense to have an ex-cop in your corner to sniff them out. On top of that Andy had a degree in business administration, and managed to add a new dimension to my career because he thought long term. He put deals together which were an investment for the future, seeds designed to flower three or four years down the line. Once I saw how he took to the work and the respect he got I trusted his judgement totally. It seemed like he was truly the man I'd dreamt of, the guy who'd swoop into my life to take care of me and give me time to do nothing, time to savour what I had. I counted my blessings.

Not that Andy gave me too much time, not at all. In our kitchen was a blackboard and on it he wrote 'Nina will be a rich black bitch by . . .' The last part was always changing; he'd write 'Xmas '63' on it until November 1963 when he'd replace it with 'Easter '65' or some other mythical deadline. That date was the day we would retire, fat and rich, and never work again. It was the reason we toured eight months of the year and recorded while we were off the road, the reason I was tired every night, and the reason why I would look out of a hotel window sometimes and see something on the street, any little thing, and start to cry. And it was the reason why, when I felt like that, I'd try to shrug it off and keep on working, earning the money to make it to our Promised Land.

Through the early sixties I went from being a New York name to a national star and then on to international fame. Andy deserves the credit for most of that. Getting stardom and, once you've got it, keeping it, is like fighting a war. You plan your campaign, recruit your troops, equip them properly and then fight until you've stormed the cities you want. Then you dig in and defend your position. Andy was our general: by 1964 he had everything in place, with a full-time office at 507 5th Avenue in New York where our press agent and business manager worked, along with their assistants. Max Cohen handled the legal details. We had three cars – the Mercedes, a Lincoln for touring and a big shooting-brake for the musicians. When we hit the road it was a slick operation, from car to hotel to concert hall to car to hotel to airport and on and on for days at a time, with press interviews and TV and radio appearances slotted in between. Andy planned it all, and it ran like clockwork.

I'd been making a living from music on my own for ten years, and sharing the load came as an enormous relief. So when Andy set up different companies to separate the recording, songwriting and performing aspects of my work I sat back happily and let him do it: it seemed the natural and right thing to do. At the back of all we did in business was the fact that he was the husband and I was the wife and ours was a traditional marriage; if at the end of the day the husband said 'This is how it will be', then that's how it was. I signed no contracts because Andy did that for me; I received no royalty cheques because they went into the companies Andy controlled on my behalf; and I had no private bank account because if I needed money for anything I asked Andy and he gave it to me. There wasn't even a joint account in both our names: if someone had asked me how much money I had back then I would have said 'Ask Andy', because there was no way I could have known.

I didn't question these arrangements because I needed Andy so much. He was the one person who held me together when things got bad. Out on the road sometimes I would drink in the way you take an aspirin, as a means of pushing the pain away in order to keep going. If ever that looked like going too far Andy would step in, pour the bourbon down the sink and hold me, tell me stories, spend time with me, help me to relax. Singing disturbed me in a way I had never experienced with classical music; the tunes stayed in my head for hours – sometimes days – at a time, and I couldn't sleep or even simply calm down. When I came off the road it took as long as a week before the music slipped away completely and I felt halfway normal again. On tour it was always going round in my head, and any rest I got was in short bursts before my brain struck up again and I was jerked awake. A person in that sort of state reaches out for anything that might take the pain away and musicians have their own antidotes for these sorts of problems – some with dangerous side-effects of their own and many of them illegal. Andy knew me well enough to understand what I was going through and he protected me then, when I was at my most vulnerable. He was my cop.

We had hardly settled into Mount Vernon before I became pregnant. We had built a three-room nursery on the top floor of the house, with two rooms for the baby and one for a nurse, but even though I had planned to get pregnant its suddenness was a surprise. Andy was delighted at the idea of being a father again, and I loved being pregnant because of how it made him feel. I didn't care too much for the discomfort – I was sick all the time and the slightest smell of tobacco would send me running from the room – but Andy had seen it all before and took it with his usual ease. When I got cravings for pickles and strawberries he'd drive into town in the middle of the night to fetch some without a murmur. But even though I grew bigger every day the blackboard in the kitchen still wove its spell and I worked up until the last six weeks. Colpix released a new album then, *Nina Sings Ellington*, with my picture on the cover. I was eight months gone: the photographer tried all sorts of tricks to hide my size but none of them worked, so they used a close-up of my face cropped out of a full-length shot and that's the picture on the sleeve even today.

I carried my baby for more than nine months and towards the end was very uncomfortable; I couldn't hold my water and had to carry a jar with me everywhere I went. When I was due my sister Frances came up from Philadelphia to stay. There were one or two false alarms and Andy, for all his experience, was getting a little nervous. One afternoon we were round at a friend's house when I started to feel ill again. We called our doctor to tell him what was going on and the doctor said it sounded like another false alarm. At that moment Frances walked in, took a look at me and said, 'Andy, I don't care what that doctor thinks – that baby's coming today.' He put me in the Mercedes – I was praying we'd get to the hospital in time and not mess up my beautiful leather upholstery – and put his police driving skills to work. We made it to the hospital in record time and they rushed me to the delivery room, Andy at my side.

Our child, a daughter, was born forty-five minutes later. It was the 12 September 1962, three years to the day since I had played my debut concert at Town Hall, and if anyone had given me a choice during the birth I would have jumped onstage and played for a week rather than have to endure another minute of labour. It hurt like hell; I swear I thought I was going to die. But amid the pain I suddenly heard my child crying and I turned to Andy. 'How's the baby?' I said. He looked at me and replied 'How's the mother?' I loved him for that.

We named her Lisa Celeste. Andy was especially thrilled with a daughter, because one of his other daughters had died very early after accidentally drinking poison and he had never really got over the tragedy. She had been called Celeste, so we named Lisa after her. Even though I had been carrying her for so long, Lisa's birth was a miraculous event to me. Oh God, I loved her. The hours after she was born I felt like a feather and loved the world and everything in it. To hold her in my arms . . .

After three weeks they released us from hospital and we went back to Mount Vernon and the new nursery. Rose Steward, my baby nurse, was waiting there and we settled into an easy routine. I had intended to breastfeed Lisa but Andy didn't want me to, he was jealous – I quite liked that. We spent our first Christmas as a family preparing for our long-delayed wedding celebration, a cruise to Acapulco. There were a few raised eyebrows on deck that January when we told our fellow passengers that the three of us – Andy, Lisa and I – were on honeymoon.

Lisa's birth was my first long period away from performance since I had started singing, and the break came as a relief. Events in my life had moved so fast since the Town Hall concert that I needed some time to sit back and think about it all, and having to stay at home with Lisa made that possible. The responsibility of being a parent forces you to look at things differently anyway, so as well as thinking about the future and trying to map it out with Andy, I started to take a more direct interest in the world around me, this world I had brought a child into.

It was a new experience for me. Most of my life I had been working towards intensely private goals with a dedication which excluded everything else. I had turned down boyfriends, marriage proposals and any chance of a happy life outside of music. I had lost Edney Whiteside, a great love. Then my rise to stardom came along almost by accident, and as I acquired fame and money those early goals I had chased so hard slowly slipped away. Classical music became a part of my past almost without my realizing it: there just wasn't the time to practise any more, or the motivation. That intense young black girl who once burned with an ambition to play in front of an orchestra at Carnegie Hall was now a wife and mother with a career to take care of and employees and their families to support. People relied on me: if I quit whenever I felt like it then my musicians and staff, many of them good friends, would suffer. I looked at the organization Andy had built around my talent and realized I was way beyond the point where I could turn back. One day on a flight between Los Angeles and New York I worked out that there were thirty-seven people – not including my own family – depending on me getting on stage that night in order that they would get paid. I began to understand the responsibilities I had.

At the same time I started to pay closer attention to what was happening in my country, especially to the advances my own people were making with the civil rights movement. I had not made a connection between the fights I had and any wider struggle for justice because of how I was raised: the Waymon way was to turn away from prejudice and to live your life as best you could, as if acknowledging the existence of racism was in itself a kind of defeat. That was what I did after Curtis: I turned away from the disgrace I felt after being refused the scholarship and pursued my ambition from a different angle. Of course I knew discrimination existed, but I didn't allow myself to admit it had any effect on me.

Like anyone with half a brain I had followed the development of the civil rights movement from its early days with Rosa Parks and Martin Luther King Junior and the Montgomery bus boycott in 1955. Watching the way the protest in Montgomery grew from one black woman's determination to sit, just once, in the front of a public bus, to a city-wide black boycott of public services, a boycott which survived for well over a year in the face of brutal intimidation, I understood for the first time the power of collective action. But I didn't make the jump to thinking I had a part to play in what was happening. Through knowing black leaders as friends right from my very early days in New York I was always aware of what the vanguard of black artists and thinkers were concerned with, but I wasn't an activist in any sense; I heard the conversations flow around me at Langston's or in the Blue Note with Jimmy Baldwin; I laughed at the political jokes at the Village Gate and a political awareness seeped into me without my having even to think about it. But I wasn't taking the trouble to educate myself in an organized way – where would I find the time? It would take a special kind of friend really to pull me into the ideas of the Black Movement and force me to accept that I had to take politics seriously.

That special friend was Lorraine Hansberry, the first black writer to have a hit Broadway play – *Raisin in the Sun* in 1958 – and the person who first took me out of myself and allowed me to see the bigger picture. I was introduced to Lorraine in the early sixties, but I only got to know her well after I moved to Mount Vernon. Lorraine lived about ten miles away in Quilton on the Hudson. We started to visit each other all the time and became firm friends. She was Lisa's godmother and gave her a beautiful silver Tiffany hairbrush and comb for her christening present. Although Lorraine was a girlfriend – a friend of my own, rather than one shared with Andy – we never talked about men or clothes or other such inconsequential things when we got together. It was always Marx, Lenin and revolution – real girls' talk.

Lorraine was most definitely an intellectual, and saw civil rights as only one part of the wider racial and class struggle. She understood that I felt separated from what was going on, but told me over and over that like it or not I was involved in the struggle by the fact of being black – it made no difference whether I admitted it or not, the fact was still true. Lorraine was truly dedicated: although she loved beautiful things, she denied them to herself because they would distract her from the struggle, which was her life. She wore no make-up except lipstick, and had only five dresses. 'I'm pretty the way I am,' she'd say, 'I don't need lots of clothes.'

Lorraine started off my political education, and through her I started thinking about myself as a black person in a country run by white people and a woman in a world run by men. I realized I was ignorant and had much to learn, but my teachers from Lorraine onwards were the cream of the movement: Stokely Carmichael, Godfrey Cambridge and many, many others, most of whom I would never meet face to face but in their writings, speeches or just in their actions. Like Rosa Parks when she sat in the front of that bus in Montgomery and refused to move, no matter what – they pointed the way forward.

Like so many people dedicated to the stuggle for freedom in America Lorraine died before her time. Cancer killed her when she was just thirty-four, only a couple of years after Lisa's christening. When she was getting ready to die she asked for me, and I went down to the hospital with a record player. I played 'In the Evening by the Moonlight' for her, and she raised her hands in front of her face and said 'Nina, I don't know what's happening to me. They say I'm not going to get better, but I must get well. I must go down to the south. I've been a revolutionary all my life, but I've got to go down there to find out what kind of revolutionary I am.' She never got out of that hospital, and the next time I played 'In the Evening by the Moonlight' was at her funeral service in New York. I didn't cry; I was beyond crying by that time. Before she died Lorraine had been working on a new play, *To Be Young, Gifted and Black*. I took the title and wrote a song around it in memory of Lorraine, and of so many others.

> To be young, gifted and black,
> Oh what a lovely precious dream.
> To be young, gifted and black,
> Open your heart to what I mean.
> In the whole world you know
> There are a billion boys and girls
> Who are young, gifted and black,
> And that's a fact!

In early 1963, as I nursed Lisa, all that was still to come. Dr King's Southern Christian Leadership Conference was deep into another campaign in Birmingham, Alabama, using the issue of desegregating the downtown lunch counters to politicize and educate the whole community. On Good Friday, Dr King was arrested while praying in the streets of Birmingham. At the same time I set out for Chicago to play a date at the Sutherland Lounge. Dr King was writing his famous Letter from Birmingham Jail while I was on stage. When I got back to Mount Vernon Lorraine called to point out the comparison and asked what was I doing for the movement while its leaders were stuck in jail. Later Dr King was released, and soon afterwards the city of Birmingham gave in to the SCLC's demands. I thought an important victory had been won, and when a little while later President Kennedy announced he was going to present a new Civil Rights Bill to Congress it seemed like another was on the way.

The President's announcement was on 11 June. The very next night, while Kennedy was on TV talking about the 'moral crisis' in America, Medgar Evers – a field secretary for the NAACP in Jackson, Mississippi – was shot to death on the steps of his home. I heard the news with disgust, but it seemed like just one more bitter news story at a time when there were already too many. At the trial of the white man accused of Medgar Evers' murder, the Governor of Mississippi walked into the courthouse to shake hands with the man in the dock. I noted this at the time, but didn't react to it – I was still turning the other cheek. What I didn't appreciate was that, while Medgar Evers' murder was not the final straw for me, it was the match that lit the fuse.

In September I started to prepare myself for our first tour since Lisa's birth. I was to start a week at the Village Gate on the 20th of the month and then fly to Los Angeles for further concerts. In Mount Vernon we had a little apartment built over the garage which was my private hideaway, where I went to practise and prepare for forthcoming performances. I was sitting there in my den on 15 September when news came over the radio that somebody had thrown dynamite into the 16th Street Baptist Church in Birmingham, Alabama while black children were attending a Bible study class. Four of them – Denise McNair, Cynthia Wesley, Carole Robertson and Addie Mae Collins – had been killed. Later that day, in the rioting which followed, Birmingham police shot another black kid and a white mob pulled a young black man off his bicycle and beat him to death, out in the street. It was more than I could take, and I sat struck dumb in my den like St Paul on the road to Damascus: all the truths that I had denied to myself for so long rose up and slapped my face. The bombing of the little girls in Alabama and the murder of Medgar Evers were like the final pieces of a jigsaw that made no sense until you had fitted the whole thing together. I suddenly realized what it was to be black in America in 1963, but it wasn't an intellectual connection of the type Lorraine had been repeating to me over and over – it came as a rush of fury, hatred and determination. In church language, the Truth entered into me and I 'came through'.

I went down to the garage and got a load of tools and junk together and took them up to my apartment. Andy came in an hour later, saw the mess and asked me what I was doing. My explanation didn't make sense because the words tumbled out in a rush – I couldn't speak quickly enough to release the torrents inside my head. He understood, though, and was still enough of a cop to see I was trying to make a zip gun, a home-made pistol. I had it in my mind to go out and kill someone, I didn't know who, but someone I could identify as being in the way of my people getting some justice for the first time in three hundred years. Andy didn't try to stop me, but just stood there for a while and said, 'Nina, you don't know anything about killing. The only thing you've got is music.' He left me alone while I calmed down enough to think straight. The idea of fighting for the rights of my people, killing for them if it came to that, didn't disturb me too much – even back then I wasn't convinced that non-violence could get us what we wanted. But Andy was right: I knew nothing about killing and I did know about music. I sat down at my piano. An hour later I came out of my apartment with the sheet music for 'Mississippi Goddam' in my hand. It was my first civil rights song, and it erupted out of me quicker than I could write it down. I knew then that I would dedicate myself to the struggle for black justice, freedom and equality under the law for as long as it took, until all our battles were won.

Once I got inside the civil rights movement I found out that many people already thought of me as a political artist, a 'protest singer', because I used to talk about civil rights on stage sometimes, praising the freedom riders, or asking if there was anyone from the SNCC – pronounced 'snick', the Student Nonviolent Co-ordinating Committee – in the house. If there was, I got them to stand up so all those who were doing nothing while these people got busted fighting for their rights felt good and guilty. But I didn't consider myself involved; I was just spurring them on as best I could from where I sat – on stage, an artist, separate somehow. That's how I felt, coming as I did from a classical background. Nightclubs were dirty, making records was dirty, popular music was dirty and to mix all that with politics seemed senseless and demeaning. And until songs like 'Mississippi Goddam' just burst out of me I had musical problems as well: how can you take the memory of a man like Medgar Evers and reduce all that he was to three and a half minutes and a simple tune? That was the musical side of it I shied away from; I didn't like 'protest music' because a lot of it was so simple and unimaginative it stripped the dignity away from the people it was trying to celebrate.

But the Alabama church bombings and the murder of Medgar Evers stopped that argument and with 'Mississippi Goddam' I realized there was no turning back. I went up to New York as planned and sang the song in public for the first time at the Village Gate. It brought the place down, and I got the same reaction wherever I sang it. We released it as a single and it sold well, except in the south, where we had trouble with distribution. The excuse was profanity – Goddam! – but the real reason was obvious enough. A dealer in South Carolina sent a whole crate of copies back to our office with each one snapped in half. I laughed, because it meant we were getting through. In some states the distributors bleeped out the word 'Goddam', changed the wording on the sleeve and released it under the title 'Mississippi #★★#!'.

After the murder of Medgar Evers, the Alabama bombing and 'Mississippi Goddam' the entire direction of my life shifted, and for the next seven years I was driven by civil rights and the hope of black revolution. I was proud of what I was doing and proud to be part of a movement that was changing history. It made what I did for a living something much more worthwhile. I had started singing because it was a way of earning more money; then fame came along and I began to enjoy the trappings of success, but after a while even they weren't enough, and I got my fulfilment outside of music – from my husband, my daughter, my home. That changed when I started singing for the movement because I justified what I was doing to myself and to the world outside, I could finally answer Momma's great unasked question, 'Why do you sing out in the world when you could be praising God?'

I needed to be able to answer that question because, although being a performing artist sounded like something grand and wonderful, up to then it felt like just another job. I didn't feel like an 'artist' because the music I played, to which I dedicated my artistry, was so inferior. That was why I put as much of my classical background as I could into the songs I performed and the music I recorded, to give it at least some depth and quality. The world of popular music was nothing compared to the classical world: you didn't have to work as hard, the audiences were too easily pleased, and all they were interested in was the delivery of the lyrics. It seemed like a nothing world to me, and I didn't have much respect for popular audiences because they were so musically ignorant.

As I became more involved in the movement this attitude I had towards my audiences changed, because I admired what they were achieving for my people so much that the level of their musical education didn't come into it any more. They gave me respect too, not only for my music – which they loved – but because they understood the stand I was making. They knew I was making sacrifices and running risks just like they were, and we were all in it together. Being a part of this struggle made me feel so good. My music was dedicated to a purpose more important than classical music's pursuit of excellence; it was dedicated to the fight for freedom and the historical destiny of my people. I felt a fierce pride when I thought about what we were all doing together. So if the movement gave me nothing else, it gave me self-respect.

It was at this time, in the mid-sixties, that I first began to feel the power and spirituality I could connect with when I played in front of an audience. I'd been performing for ten years, but it was only at this time that I felt a kind of state of grace come upon me on those occasions when everything fell into place. At such times I would give a concert that everyone who witnessed it would remember for years, and they would go home afterwards knowing that something very special had happened.

Those moments are very difficult for a performer to explain. It's like being transported in church; something descends upon you and you are gone, taken away by a spirit that is outside of you. I can only think of one comparison: I went to a bullfight in Barcelona once, not knowing what to expect. I sat in the sun drinking vodka waiting for it to begin and when they got the bull out and killed him I threw up from the mixture of alcohol and shock. It was a Sunday afternoon blood-letting, a real blood-letting. Back in Tryon at revival time people would 'come through' and shout, carry on and foam at the mouth. We'd call it 'blood-letting' but it wasn't – not real blood-letting like it was that Sunday afternoon. I realized then that Spanish people were not much different from black people in America in the Holy Roller Church, and the songs performed by the flamenco musicians were similar to those perfomed by my people in churches in the black south – all rhythm and emotion. The only difference was they actually killed the bull in Spain, whereas in America they had revival meetings where the death and sacrifice were only symbolic. But it was the same thing, the same sense of being transformed, of celebrating something deep, something very deep. That's what I learned about performing – that it was real, and I had the ability to make people *feel* on a deep level. It's difficult to describe because it's not something you can analyse; to get near what it's about you have to play it.

And when you've caught it, when you've got the audience hooked, you always know because it's like electricity hanging in the air. I began to feel it happening and it seemed to me like mass hypnosis – like I was hypnotizing an entire audience to feel a certain way. I was the toreador mesmerizing this bull and I could turn around and walk away, turning my back on this huge animal which I knew would do nothing because I had it under my complete control. And, like they did with the toreadors, people came to see me because they knew I was playing close to the edge and one day I might fail. This was how

I got my reputation as a live performer, because I went out from the mid-sixties onwards determined to get every audience to enjoy my concerts the way I wanted them to, and if they resisted at first I had all the tricks to bewitch them with.

I know it all sounds a little Californian and wired, but it wasn't like that at all: I had technique, and I used it. To cast the spell over an audience I would start with a song to create a certain mood which I carried into the next song and then on through into the third, until I created a certain climax of feeling and by then they would be hypnotized. To check, I'd stop and do nothing for a moment and I'd hear absolute silence: I'd got them. It was always an uncanny moment. It was as if there was a power source somewhere that we all plugged into, and the bigger the audience the easier it was – as if each person supplied a certain amount of the power. As I moved on from clubs into bigger halls I learned to prepare myself thoroughly: I'd go to the empty hall in the afternoon and walk around to see where the people were sitting, how close they'd be to me at the front and how far away at the back, whether the seats got closer together or further apart, how big the stage was, how the lights were positioned, where the microphones were going to hit – everything. I was especially careful of microphones, taking the trouble to find one that worked for me and throwing away those that didn't. So by the time I got on stage I knew exactly what I was doing.

Before important concerts I would practise alone for hours at a time, so long sometimes that my arms would seize up completely. There was one period when I was so dissatisfied with drummers that I decided not to use them any more. So I sat down for days and trained my left hand like a drum; just as I mastered it my arm went paralysed from all the work it had done. Other times I'd fall asleep at the piano and Andy would have to come and put me to bed. I made sure the musicians in my bands understood in every detail the way we were to play and we rehearsed regularly, but the vital thing was that they empathized with me and understood the way I was likely to go on stage. My ideal musician was Al Schackman, but there were others who were almost as wonderful – and those that weren't got fired on day one. My bands knew the repertoire of songs I would choose from, but I never gave them a set list until the very last minute – sometimes as we walked out on stage – because the songs I played each night depended on the mood I caught from the audience, the hall and my preparations through the day. When I walked out to play I was super-sensitive and, whilst aware of the crowd, tried to play for myself, have a good time and hope the audience would get pulled into that, as if – like my musicians – they were an extension of me for the time the concert lasted.

The saddest part of performing was – and still is – that it didn't mean anything once you were off stage. I never felt proud of being a performer or got vain about it, because it mostly came naturally and I didn't feel that I completely understood or controlled what happened on stage anyhow. I did my preparations as carefully as possible in order to set the scene, but having done that the rest was difficult to predict. I knew the songs to play, and in what order, but the difference between a good professional performance and a great show, one where I would get lost in the music, was impossible to know. It just happened. Whatever it was that happened out there under the lights, it mostly came from God, and I was just a place along the line He was moving on. With civil rights I played on stage for a reason, and when I walked off stage those reasons still existed – they didn't fade away with the applause; and there were always new ideas to discuss, articles to read, speakers to listen to and songs to write. For the first time performing made sense as a part of my life – it was no longer that strange and wonderful two hours out front which only depressed you more when you got back to the dressing room and stared at the paint peeling off the walls and wondered if you'd get any sleep that night.

As my commitment deepened and I started to play benefits, go on marches and mix with a wide range of people involved in civil rights, I got to hear stories about what I meant to some of these activists, and what I heard astonished me. I was always most sympathetic to SNCC, which was made up of younger people, students mainly, and had risen up spontaneously in 1960 around a series of sit-ins in segregated diners in Greensboro, South Carolina. The attitude of the people in SNCC was the closest to how I felt – that there was more than one way to skin a cat and whatever means worked to get what you wanted was the right one to use. Like SNCC, I felt non-violence was the way forward in the early sixties because it seemed to get results, but I wasn't committed to non-violence for ideological reasons like Dr King's organization, the SCLC. I knew a time might come where we would have to fight for what was right, and I had no problem with that: the Ku Klux Klan weren't non-violent, and neither were the police, nor the government if they felt threatened.

My friends in SNCC told me that when they got started and had their meetings to discuss strategy – meetings which often turned into parties later – there would always be Nina Simone records in whoever's house the meeting was held in. In 1962 – I heard this years later – some SNCC guys from Howard University in Washington went to a conference in Nashville and were astonished to find their Tennessee comrades had the exact same records of mine as they did! The Washington members had thought Nina Simone was their own private discovery, but everywhere they went to meet fellow workers they found my records. In 1964 SNCC had a conference in Atlanta which was fixed for a certain date until the Mississippi delegation wrote saying that, as I was coming to play at the Magnolia Ballroom two weeks later, they wanted the conference date switched so they could get to see me and go to the conference at the same time. So they switched the date.

Other SNCC people told me proudly that the only thing that ever got stolen from their offices – meaning the only things SNCC workers stole from each other – were books and Nina Simone records, and that the only thing guaranteed to make members forget their non-violent training was for them to find out their Nina Simone records were missing.

When I started to hear these stories – and much of this was happening before Medgar Evers was killed and the church bombed – I realized that the whole time I'd been in New York struggling to come to terms with my career, and all those afternoons when Lorraine had been telling me there was a struggle going on which I had to get involved in, I had been involved anyway. Those kids out in the backwoods knew I was a part of their fight before I knew it myself, and when I finally met up with them, the 'stormtroopers of the movement' who didn't have the protection of fame, money and a comfortable home like I did, who risked their lives every day, it convinced me further that I had no choice but to line up alongside them. You can call it what you like, but to me it seemed like destiny.

Chapter 7

The fight for civil rights hadn't sprung up with Dr King and the Montgomery bus boycott; it had been around since slavery days, and the movement I knew was the latest version of that struggle. Like all newcomers to it, the first thing I had to do was educate myself in my own history and understand the reasons why I should be proud of my own culture.

I read, or was told, about the great black nations of Africa – Benin, Egypt, Nigeria, all over – about how black civilizations had existed while Europe was still in the Dark Ages, and the days when the only civilized peoples in North America were the native Indians who had yet to suffer the white man. I was guided by Langston, who sometimes gave me books he thought I should read, but more often simply sat me down and told me what I should know. I'd go over to his place in Harlem and over dinner – southern style – we'd talk, recite songs and poems and drink wine until the sun came up. Then I'd catch a cab home, high on wine, music and laughter.

At the end of 1963 it wasn't simply a question of being 'for' civil rights. By then many of the aims that the movement had fought for in the fifties looked like they were on the way: the Civil Rights Act was made law in July 1964, and the Voting Rights Act in 1965. We knew that just because the rights we demanded were protected by Federal Law, it didn't mean those laws would automatically be applied in every state. But the hopes of those early years looked like coming true, and the question everyone was asking was: 'Where do we go from here?'

We weren't one unified group agreeing on everything and moving together (although to read the press anyone would think we were a single army marching behind Dr King); we were a whole range of people thinking, discussing and arguing among ourselves. There were my friends at SNCC, who liked to organize from the ground up and who distrusted Dr King's SCLC with its leaders in Atlanta telling local communities what they should do; there was CORE, the Congress of Racial Equality, in Chicago, with its own structure, its own commanders, its own agenda; there was was the NAACP, the old guard, looking on at these newcomers with a – sometimes – cynical eye.

There was a lot to understand for somebody who just wanted to get involved, but it was especially important that I did: I was asked political questions in press interviews, my opinion was quoted concerning news events, and I received dozens of requests to play benefits and appear on marches. So I had to be familiar with the issues, and know who the benefits were aiding, what the marches were for and who they were organized by. If I didn't, then I might find myself marching for, say, CORE, in a campaign over a certain issue which, say, SNCC, opposed because they thought the tactics were wrong, or the timing was wrong, or the campaign aims were too vague. In the early years of civil rights these political groups had worked together, but by the mid-sixties that was happening less often. I only had a certain amount of energy and time available – Andy was trying to keep my music industry career on track while all this was going on, there were tours and recording sessions to be done, and there was still my baby daughter to look after – so I had to use whatever time there was to full effect.

My natural instinct was to agree to whatever was asked of me and leave things to sort themselves out later. I was not cold and intellectual about campaigning, I was intuitive, and when injustice stared me in the face I struck out fiercely, without taking time to consider the implications.

One time in New York I went to see an off-Broadway play with Bill Dukes and Brock Peters – two fine black actors – in the cast. I thought the roles they played were insulting to black people, and I got up there on stage in the middle of the show and told them so. I stopped the play in its tracks to ask them why they were doing trash like that. One of them said something about needing the money, but that was no excuse. They apologised, and took me home in a cab. I was half-crazy with anger that night, a woman on fire, and that was how I felt most of the time as I watched my people struggling for their rightful place in America.

I wasn't the only one torn with an impatience to get what was mine, but sometimes it felt that way. I was lucky that I had Langston, Andy, Lorraine and others around to help me. The most important among these people, and my special friend, was Stokely Carmichael. I'd met Stokely in 1962 in a church in Philadelphia; he was giving a speech and I was urged to hear him by another special new friend, Miriam Makeba. A few months earlier I'd seen her show at the Blue Angel, went backstage to say hello, and within a few minutes we felt we'd known each other all our lives. Miriam told me she'd heard my records on the radio in South Africa at the end of the fifties – which astonished me – and had wanted to meet me ever since. I loved her music the moment I heard it, but once I knew her I loved her more. It was her attitude I liked more than anything; she was so straightforward in what she said and thought, and at the same time so relaxed, so African. We had the same taste in everything: we liked the same food, drinks, men, jokes, clothes – you name it.

So Miriam told me about Stokely, and I went down to Philadelphia to meet him. He was with SNCC at the time and already well known, although nowhere near as famous as he would later become. He was talking politics and civil rights in that church, but for me, like for most women, politics wasn't what sprung straight to mind when I first laid eyes on him. He stood up to speak and I thought he had to be the most handsome man in America; judging by the fanning in the audience I wasn't alone in my opinion. He was tall, lean, had beautiful skin, bright eyes and a wonderful laughing voice.

Stokely knew I was in the audience and he pointed me out, saying I was the true singer of the civil rights movement. The way he said it, honouring me in front of those people, made me break down and cry. He made a convert of me there and then, and I would have walked into the fires of hell with him and never looked back once. After that first meeting I used to see him often: he'd come to watch me play, or I'd catch him at a march or a rally. I kept inviting him to dinner but he never came. He was so busy with his work for SNCC and he'd call up at the last minute to say sorry and promise the next time, the next time . . . he'd apologise with exquisite charm, knowing he'd already been forgiven before he had to ask.

Like all the leaders in the vanguard of the movement, Stokely was thinking about this question of where to go next. It was a great debate that was going on all around me, and after listening to various opinions I realized the first thing I had to sort out personally was whether I believed in integration or separatism. I loved Dr King for his goodness and compassion and – like everyone else – marvelled at his speech during the March on Washington. But those words, in August 1963, came just eighteen days before the four young girls were blown to pieces in their church in Birmingham. Much as I liked the idea of the world being as one and wanted it to be true, the more I looked around, the more I learned, and the less I thought it would ever happen. It was the black Moslems, led by Malcolm X, whose talk of self-reliance and self-defence seemed to echo the distrust of white America that I was feeling.

I had never met Malcolm X face-to-face, although I did hear him speak in Harlem more than once, but I knew his wife, Betty Shabaz, because she was a neighbour of ours in Mount Vernon. She had been moving here and there with her children after Malcolm left Elijah Mohammed and the Nation of Islam because he felt he was moving in a different direction, politically and spiritually, from the Moslem movement that had spawned him. Then Malcolm was murdered and a group of people came together to raise the money for Betty to find a place, and I got involved in that.

A while later I met Louis Farrakhan too, through a friend of mine who had converted, Pearl Reynolds Bryce. Reverend Farrakhan sent a message through her that I was his favourite singer and that my song 'Consummation' was his all-time favourite. He invited me to meet him at a temple in New York, so I had a special hat and dress made for the occasion and went along. We chatted a little and I invited him home with me. We got back to Mount Vernon and he sat in the living room and started talking about separatism, Islam and the need to convert the whole of black America to his way of thinking. He talked for hours and I sat across from him, drinking gin and nodding my head, trying to take it all in.

The night got longer, the gin took effect and I got a little distracted, especially by his feet, which were tiny. I'd never seen feet that small and I wondered if his mother had bound them when he was a baby like the Chinese used to do with their daughters. Minister Farrakhan talked on into the small hours and I sat staring at his shoes, sipping my gin and wondering what he'd say if I invited him upstairs. He kept giving me these looks as if he knew what I was thinking. At last I couldn't stand it any longer and came out and asked him. It was more out of mischief than anything else, but he spoilt the fun by turning me down; he just started talking politics again and I was too tired for that, so I sent him home. Afterwards I got messages saying he was still interested in me and would like to meet some time, but we didn't see each other again. So he didn't manage to convert me and I didn't convert him; an honourable draw. I respected him for that.

As I became more knowledgeable I came to my own conclusions about separatism. In the white man's world the black man would always lose out, so the idea of a separate black nation, whether it was in America or in Africa, made sense. But I didn't believe that there was any basic difference between the races – whoever is on top uses whatever means they can to keep the other down, and if black America was on top they'd use race as a way of oppressing whites in exactly the way they themselves were oppressed. Anyone who has power only has it at the expense of someone else and to take that power away from them you have to use force, because they'll never give it up from choice. That is what I came to believe, and it was a big step forward in my political thinking because I realized that what we were really fighting for was the creation of a new society. When I had started out in the movement all I wanted were my rights under the Constitution, but the more I thought about it the more I realized that no matter what the President or the Supreme Court might say, the only way we could get true equality was if America changed completely, top to bottom. And this change had to start with my own people, with black revolution.

These ideas developed over months and years, but in the meantime there was work in the real world to look after. Playing for the movement was always exciting, sometimes dangerous, and occasionally plain weird. In 1963 I played in the first mixed-race concert at Miles College in Birmingham, in a show supporting the desegregation campaign down there. All sorts of people were on the bill, including Johnny Mathis.

Johnny always liked to talk about how he had been a track star at college; everyone knew that if ever the conversation got round to athletics he'd bring up those days again, and it got to be something of a joke. At Miles College they had built a temporary stage using large sheets of plywood over a metal frame. As usual there had been threats made about how people would be shot if they went to the concert, or how they were going to bomb the stage and kill the artists – the sort of threats we got all the time when we played in the south.

We took those threats very seriously and it was always a funny feeling when you walked on stage, knowing that some redneck had sworn tonight would be your last show. That night Johnny was halfway through his set when the stage collapsed. The wooden boards couldn't hold the weight any more, and with a mighty crash they gave way. The first *crack* as the planks split sounded exactly like a shot from a high-velocity rifle, and people all over ducked. Then, as the stage collapsed, the second thought was that a bomb had exploded.

When the dust settled and the place calmed down everybody realized what had really happened and began to laugh. Then we looked on stage for Johnny, but he was long gone. The ex-champion athlete had heard what he thought was a rifle shot followed by what he assumed was a bomb exploding around him, and boy, did he hit the floor running! He was off that stage before anyone knew he'd even gone. The guys backstage were curled up laughing – with relief, not spite – saying, 'Hell, it's true, he was a sprinter!'

Those shows were a mixture of excitement, pride and cold, cold fear. I was playing the Village Gate in 1965 while the Selma-to-Montgomery March was going on. One afternoon Al, Art D'Lugoff and I were sitting in the club talking about it, and we decided we just had to get down there. Art cancelled the rest of our shows and we collected Andy and Langston and jumped on a plane. We came in to land at Montgomery – wheels down and everything – when the pilot suddenly pulled up and threw the plane back up in the air. We looked out of the windows and saw that bulldozers and trucks had been put out on the runway to stop our plane from landing. They had heard there were a whole load of celebrities flying in to do the show. The local authorities were determined to stop it and had blockaded the airport, ignoring the fact that airports are supposed to be under Federal control.

We diverted to Jackson, Mississippi, landed, and looked around for something to get us to Montgomery. Andy found a single-engine plane with a fat little pilot, a real cracker, who was willing to take us in. I sat up front next to the pilot, with Al and his amplifier on my other side. Andy, Art and Langston got in the back. Andy and Art were both thick-set men: as soon as they sat down their weight was too much and the plane tilted back until the tail rested on the ground and the nose pointed up in the air. It was like being on a rollercoaster while it made its first slow climb up the slope before it tumbled back down.

I looked at the pilot sitting next to me. He was chewing a big wad of gum which spilled through his teeth as he smiled and said 'Well folks, I don't think we can take off this way!' I heard Al whispering 'Holy shit' on the other side of me.

We did some rearranging and the front wheel touched ground again. The pilot said, 'Well, I think we can get off', and started the plane up. We bumped along the tarmac and halfway down the runway he said, 'Well, now I'm not so sure.' Al had his eyes shut tight and Andy just looked straight ahead, not saying a word. At last we limped into the air, cleared the fence at the airport perimeter and flew on to Montgomery, where we landed on the short runway which had been cleared of trucks.

The show was at a high school in St Jude, a little town outside of Montgomery. There were about forty thousand people waiting there, most of them having marched from Selma. The concert was in the open air and the stage was set up at one end of a soccer field, with a school bus at the side as a changing room and artists' area. Harry Belafonte was there, as well as Leonard Bernstein, Shelley Winters, and all kinds of people. The stage was another temporary construction, covered over with a big canvas apron. Everything at the show – the bus, the food, the drinks, the lights – had been donated by well-wishers. The audience got larger and larger as the marchers kept arriving, and Andy Young, later Mayor of Atlanta, but then in charge of security, was very concerned that everyone should stay together and not get separated. Out beyond the boundary of the field were woods where the police and National Guard said gangs of armed white racists were waiting, looking for an opportunity to kill someone, anyone, connected with the march.

It had been raining for much of the day and the field was covered in mud. Somehow, despite being wet, footsore and frightened, people kept their spirits together by singing and praying. They obediently followed the instructions of the security people and stood together in the rain, looking forward to the show. Performers use tired old phrases all the time and usually don't mean a word of them, but that night we all felt privileged to be playing in front of that audience.

Harry Belafonte's band were already on stage when we got there and we were due on next, so Al took his amp and set it up by the drum riser. Ralph McDonald, Harry's drummer, watched Al as he looked about for a socket to plug his amp into. Al couldn't find one so he asked Ralph, who pointed to the canvas sheet over the stage floor and said, 'You just pull up the apron and plug in underneath.' Al lifted up the apron and beneath it, supporting the stage, were dozens and dozens of empty coffins, donated by the local black mortuary to build up the stage. Al gasped, 'Oh, my God,' not believing his eyes. He looked back at Ralph, who grinned and said 'Welcome to Montgomery.'

That night when we got back to our hotel we were told to stay away from the windows. We all slept in one room with beds made up on the floor. Late in the night I looked out and on the rooftops all around our hotel were Federal marshals, with rifles, guarding us. It was some night. Langston told some stories, we sang some songs and then pretended to sleep. We flew out the next morning, exhausted.

They were crazy times for all of us, and as each day passed I looked back jealously to my early days as a star. After Lisa was born I had sworn to keep a check on the pace of my life, but in the movement I lived at twice the speed I ever had and music and politics took up my whole life. I didn't have personal ambitions any more – I wanted what millions of other Americans wanted, and enjoying any private landmarks was impossible because the outside world always managed to butt in.

On 15 January 1965 – a couple of months before Selma – I gave a concert at Carnegie Hall; the first half of the concert I performed partly solo and partly with my musicians, the second half with a full symphony orchestra. It was the sort of concert I would have killed for when I was Eunice Waymon, and even as Nina Simone it gave me enormous pleasure. Miz Mazzy was in the audience, and as I sat at the piano waiting for the orchestra to settle I looked up to where I knew she was sitting. Next to her were my parents, who I had brought up from South Carolina to see me. Daddy walked into my dressing room afterwards with pride shining out of his eyes and hugged me; Momma didn't say a word about being proud of me then, and has never mentioned it since. Miz Mazzy told me that when I wasn't around Momma did say she was proud, but she would never mention it to my face. I longed for her to say it, just once.

But even my Carnegie Hall debut couldn't pass undisturbed by the reality of our struggle. Two days before the concert I was rehearsing with the orchestra when news came through that Brother Malcolm X had been shot to death on a Harlem platform. The first thought I had was for Betty and her poor, poor children who would never grow up knowing their remarkable father. Even now I wish I had known the man. Malcolm's assassination pushed my thoughts faster down the track they were already on, that violence was going to be an inevitable part of the struggle and if we didn't understand that fast then – like I said in 'Mississippi Goddam' – we'd die like flies.

The killing was already a fact of life long before Malcolm's murder. In the six months before I played Carnegie Hall there were race riots in New York – after a ten-year-old black child was killed by police – in Jacksonville, Florida, and in Rochester, New York State. The bodies of three murdered black radicals were discovered in Philadelphia, and in the following FBI investigation five white police cadets were arrested and charged. Riots became a regular thing: Chicago exploded in the summer, followed by Philadelphia and New York again. On 15 October 1964 Dr Martin Luther King Junior received his Nobel Peace Prize: it didn't seem like there was much peace to me.

In the middle of all this Lyndon Johnson got re-elected and the war in Vietnam moved into a higher gear. It was difficult to know whether we were winning or losing because whenever anything good happened – like a civil rights bill going through Congress, or a campaign in the south ending in victory – the very next day a kid somewhere would be shot by police, or another ten thousand GIs would be shipped out to Saigon. The moment you started feeling optimistic about the way things were going, as I did at the very start of 1965, you could be sure that something terrible – like Malcolm's death – would jump up and hit you in the face.

People who lived through those times doing the same thing as I did, living and breathing revolution, will tell you the same stories of how their private lives faded away for years at a time. Nothing was personal or private. The first thing I saw in the morning when I woke up was my black face in the bathroom mirror and that fixed what I felt about myself for the rest of the day – that I was a black-skinned woman in a country where you could be killed because of that one fact. So when I left on my first European tour in the middle of the year the first thing I felt on arriving in London was relief at being away from the pressure for a while. Lisa and Andy were with me and we took time out in London before my first show. It was a beautiful summer that year in England and Andy hired bicycles so we could pedal around town like two kids on holiday. We walked through the parks in the evening and went shopping in Bond Street during the day; we did the kind of things normal tourists do and tried to kid ourselves that America didn't exist. That pretence lasted until I went on stage, when it was back to the real world again. We played London and then flew to Switzerland to do the Montreux Jazz Festival for the first time. Playing outside of the States was interesting, because my fans knew me mainly from my early records and they liked different songs from those enjoyed by my regular Stateside following.

Some really dedicated fans would ask to hear songs I had never recorded and had only played a few times in my entire life. But they knew them, and I began to realize how many times I had been bootlegged. At first I didn't mind because in some European countries it was difficult to get hold of my records, but when I found there were more bootlegs in countries like Britain and France than anywhere else I got mad; my records had always been available there from the very earliest days. In jumped the reality of my black face again: I knew that all artists were exploited in this way, but how come black artists always seemed to get ripped off more often, more extensively, than whites? Memphis Slim, whom I knew for years, never got a single penny in America from the dozens of songs published in his name. When the Rolling Stones went to Chess Records in Chicago they found Muddy Waters painting the studio wall to earn some money between recording sessions. And no sooner had black musicians got wise to the ways that small labels exploited them, than the multinational companies moved in and hid their money behind a screen of lawyers and accountants so that it took years of work and thousands of dollars just to find out how much they were stealing from you.

Throughout the tour I mixed up my repertoire and tried to play at least some of the songs the fans knew well. Until Montreux, where I sang only protest songs. I did that to make a point, to show the most prestigious music festival in Europe where I came from, what I was about, and what was happening in my country.

We got back to home in the fall only to leave again almost immediately to play Philly, Chicago and the Troubador in LA. For a couple of months I caught up with friends in between playing and then – after a week in Mount Vernon – we left for Europe again, to do a TV show in Holland, to spend a family Christmas together in London, and to catch an amazing New Year's Eve party at the house of a good friend.

The party needs explaining. By this time I had changed record companies from Colpix to Philips; although Colpix wanted to re-sign me I was seduced away by an astonishing man – Wilhelm Langenberg, known to everyone as Big Willy. I came off stage one night at the Village Gate to find this huge man who must have weighed three hundred pounds in my dressing room. I came in, saw him, said,'What the hell?' and he was off with his fantastic deep voice, booming projection, gesturing, carrying on. He said 'I'm Wilhelm Langenberg and I've come to take you back to Holland so you can be on the Philips label. I own it.' And so he did, along with his partner, Irving Green.

Big Willy had got hold of a copy of 'Mississippi Goddam' in Holland and listened to it non-stop for fifty-two hours. Then, without saying anything to his wife, he walked out of the house and caught the next plane to New York to sign me up. The way he put it there was no question about whether I was going to sign, and sure enough he negotiated a deal with Andy, tied up the loose ends with Colpix and I became a Philips artist. At least that was the way it was presented to the world; everyone in Philips knew I was a Wilhelm Langenberg artist, and I never dealt with anyone but him.

Big Willy was a man of enormous appetites and everything in his life was outsize, including his New Year's Eve parties. He and his wife Ena threw one every year that lasted for two days and damn near killed all the guests. They were the kind of parties it was worth crossing the Atlantic to get to, and apart from being fun they were educational – everything I know about drinking I learned from Big Willy at New Year's Eve. Not that Big Willy needed an excuse to have a good time, he couldn't live any other way. Once he and Irving Green took me, Andy, Ena, Quincy Jones and his wife Oolah out for dinner to a beachside restaurant in Juan-les-Pins in the south of France. The meal lasted for four hours, with Big Willy and Irving competing to see who could eat the most. At the end there were so many bones on the table it looked like an elephants' graveyard, but Big Willy and Irving were still feeling restless. So they got up, went outside, and pushed some poor guy's car off the quayside into the sea and then sat on the beach crying with laughter as it slowly filled up with water.

Like many large men Big Willy could also be wonderfully gentle and sensitive, for all his noise and bluster. We were recording in Holland once when Andy got angry with me over something and Big Willy stepped in and said, 'Andy, look at you, you have no deep sense of your colour – you don't really know who you are. Nina has colour and she has the weight of forty million people on her back. You know, you should be gentle with her.' I don't know who was more shocked, Andy or me. No one had ever shown they understood me like that before, no black person, no American, and here was this Dutch Orson Welles who cut straight to what I was in a couple of sentences.

We went back to Big Willy's every New Year for ten years and he and Ena were our greatest friends in Europe. There was a standing joke between us that we had married the wrong people; I should have married Big Willy, and Andy, Ena. Not such a bad idea, I sometimes thought.

Without knowing it, Big Willy helped save me from myself because, as the sixties went on and America turned on the movement and destroyed it, I became bitter and disillusioned. Years of hope turned to despair – like I said, at Lorraine's funeral I was long past crying – and sometimes despair turned to hate of all things white. At times like that it was the thought of men like Wilhelm Langenberg which saved me from bigotry, because he was impossible to hate. I guess I loved him; he was the greatest friend a person could have. I can still say that today, even though after he died I found out something that might have torn our friendship apart: the whole time he knew me, and released my records on his label, he was involved in a company which made and sold ships to the South African government.

I was shocked when I was told that, but it helped to solve a mystery that had puzzled me. Some time after I split up with Andy I went to Holland to see Big Willy. I was very down, very sick of my country, and very lonely. My old friend invited me to dinner, made me laugh, and then came back to my hotel room for a final drink. When we got inside I got to my knees and bared my breasts, took my dress down and said 'I've come to marry you, because you always said that you should marry me if I wasn't married to Andy.'

Big Willy got down there with me, held my hand and said, 'Madam,' – he always called me that – 'Madam, when you all take over I will be dead, but I will come back and I will be the gardener, but I will only take care of the roses.' Then he lifted my dress back up and left. I never saw him again because he died a few months later, while I was on tour. He was fifty-two years old.

I had wondered what Big Willy meant about 'when you all take over I'll be dead', and it was only when I heard about his South African ships that I realized what he was talking about. What he was actually saying was he wouldn't marry me for reasons he couldn't say at that moment but which I would understand later. He knew his secret would always come between us and for that alone we could never marry – not because he thought I would find out, but because he knew more than anyone what a wrong thing he had done. Big Willy couldn't marry me knowing that about himself; he was too decent a man.

The way I found out about his death shows the casual horror of a performer's life. I was out on the road and I hadn't been home for months; I hadn't been in any one place for more than a few days and my mail was chasing me around the world, arriving at hotels the day after I left, being forwarded and missing me and being forwarded again. Ena had written to me in America, but somehow her letter never got sent on. What I did receive was a card from Philips, but by this time I wasn't recording for them any more and anyhow it was in Dutch. It wasn't signed by Willy and I thought it was some sort of greeting card – just a company circular saying hello – so I put it in my bag and forgot about it. A little while later I was in my dressing room after a show and the place was full of fans, reporters and photographers. One of the journalists was Dutch, and I remembered the card and gave it to him to translate for me. He glanced at it and read 'Wilhelm Langenberg has died.' Time stopped: I felt as if I was turning to stone and sat dumbly shaking hands and signing autographs, alone in a crowded room. I had missed his funeral, missed the wonderful party afterwards that he would have loved and now I was in the middle of a tour, about to try to sleep – alone – in a strange hotel in a strange city three thousand miles from home.

Back in the States after that first Christmas in London and Big Willy's party I wanted to meet up with Stokely and my other friends in the movement in order to catch up with the latest news. I managed to do that almost straightaway, because I was booked to play at a CORE fundraiser in Chicago in the middle of January. I thought it was going to be a normal benefit until I arrived at O'Hare Airport – in the freezing cold – to be told that I was to receive a CORE citation for my work in the movement. It was a kind gesture, and I appreciated it, but the news that really made me glow was that at the same ceremony 'Young, Gifted and Black' was going to be declared the 'National Anthem of Black America'. I wasn't in the movement for personal glory, but this dedication made me very proud because it showed I was succeeding as a protest singer, that I was writing songs people remembered and were inspired by. It was a beautiful evening, with everyone singing and moving together, digging the music, empowered. When I walked into the hall there was one final surprise waiting: the DJ for the show was Sid Marx, the guy who had broken 'Porgy' on air in Philly and had started my whole damn ball rolling. He stood grinning at me like a fool and the past ten years of my life flashed before me, from piano bars to revolutionary fundraisers, obscurity to fame. I didn't know whether to kiss him or kill him.

Stokely, meantime, had been working out his answer to the 'where do we go from here' question; he and Huey Newton combined all sorts of related ideas about economics, social justice and political resistance under the general heading of 'Black Power'. I talked to Stokely and read their manifesto. I agreed with every word: I just wish some of the opponents of Black Power had bothered to read it too, because they would have understood that Black Power was a lot more than black men with guns – it was a way of returning the black man's pride.

When you mention Black Power people automatically think of the Black Panthers, but although the Panthers evolved out of these ideas, they were only part of the overall philosophy. A good part, though; I thanked God for them, because they showed young blacks who thought the only means of protest was passive non-violence that there was another way, that they didn't have to take all the mental and physical cruelty inflicted on them by whites. With the arrival of the Panthers black kids realized there were black heroes who would fight and die if necessary to make sure they got what they wanted. I thought that was wonderful. They scared the hell out of white folks too, and we certainly needed that; we needed to show that our goodwill could not be taken for granted any more.

In May 1966 Stokely was voted in as chairman of SNCC. When it was founded in 1960 SNCC had pledged itself to non-violence, so Stokely's election shows how much it had changed over six years. Two months after Stokely's election the CORE congress in Chicago adopted the concept of Black Power, three days later the NAACP disassociated itself from SNCC and – by implication – from the decision of the CORE congress. Dr King and the SCLC were, of course, non-violent and exclusively Christian. The main organizations of the movement were making different decisions about the right way forward, reflecting the uncertainty many people felt. I knew that the right way – at that moment – lay with Stokely, Black Power and the Panthers. A month after CORE adopted Black Power, Dr King was stabbed while marching in Chicago. That day I was playing an open-air concert at the skating rink in New York's Central Park when the news came through on the radio. I was tired of our leaders having to risk their lives each time they went out on the street, tired of being asked to turn the other cheek each time my race was subjected to another indignity. I, for one, was through with turning the other cheek, through with loving my enemies. It was time for some Old Testament justice.

As 1966 drew to a close the mood in New York, Chicago, Atlanta, LA – all the big cities I played in – became more militant and less forgiving. A few thought American society would change, that the revolution would happen, but more often people just acknowledged that for the movement the hard times were getting close. I spent the final weeks of the year preparing for a nationwide tour opening for Bill Cosby, knowing that no matter what happened elsewhere I would be tied to my tour itinerary for the duration.

For me, the Cosby tour was a sign of things to come. As we set out for the first show I felt tired, but I'd felt tired for the last twelve years so I thought nothing of it. For all my exhaustion I couldn't sleep properly, and my head was filled with music and snatches from speeches or conversations from the past two years. At odd moments my mind would leave entirely and I'd sit staring at nothing, unaware of time going by until some noise snapped me out of it.

The first few dates went well. Bill Cosby was wonderful, both as a comedian, at which he was great – and great every night, which is the hard part – and as a headliner and touring partner. He treated me well. The problems started when Andy walked into my dressing room and found me staring into the mirror putting make-up in my hair, brown make-up, because I wanted to be the same colour all over. I was wearing a white gown and all I could think about was how the colour of my gown should contrast with the rest of me, which had to be the same all over.

Andy came in and looked at me and I saw from his eyes that he was very worried about something. I was in a state where I was half outside myself, observing my peculiar behaviour from a safe distance. Andy looked scared.

'Don't tell Bill!' was the first thing I said to him. 'Don't tell Bill!' So

Andy tried to talk me through it and calm me down, but I kind of drifted away from him. He tried to get me to talk sense, but I said things like he wasn't my husband, he was my nephew, and we were going to fly back up to heaven together and he'd better do what I said because I was Grandma Moses. At the same time wave after wave of tiredness broke over me and I felt like any minute I would fall asleep for a hundred years. I looked over at Andy and for a moment I could see right through his skin, right through as if he were covered in plastic, and I saw the blood pushing around, and the organs of his body twitching and throbbing, his heart beating. And then it was gone, and I was near to my normal self again.

Andy was frightened and asked me if I wanted to quit the tour and go home, but we were over halfway through and I didn't want to let everyone down, especially Bill. So we carried on, and the weirdness carried on too, coming and going. I had visions of laser beams and heaven, with skin – always skin – involved in there somewhere. My waking hours were a succession of intense daydreams with short calm periods in between.

On stage I was lost completely but my subconscious got on with the show and no one noticed the difference except my musicians and Andy, who stood anxiously in the wings wondering if I was about to faint or say something really crazy. Every now and then my music was altered by these moods – once I found myself playing the *Lone Ranger* theme music, very softly and quietly – but it was mostly my perceptions, how I saw the world.

Between us, Andy and I, we got through it and finished the tour. When we arrived back in Mount Vernon I slept for three solid days and nights.

Andy sighed with relief. For a moment he thought I had gone crazy and would have to go to hospital or undergo analysis. He thought he might have lost me. If I'd thought about it at all I suppose I would have realized it was some kind of warning, but once I felt better I didn't consider it worth thinking about: there was too much happening to get sick now. It was like Lorraine had said: I had to find out what kind of revolutionary I was, and the revolution – or something like it – was on its way.

Chapter 8

The Cosby tour finished in February 1967 and we left on a short tour of Europe almost immediately, giving me very little time to rest. I didn't want to go, not because I felt too tired – I always felt too tired – but because the political scene was moving so fast I was frightened of missing something while I was away. There was a general feeling among us that the time for revolution was ripe, and if we didn't work all out to make it happen we might not get another shot at it for years. It was a funny thing, but the more difficult and dangerous the fight became the more optimistic I felt. We had left the old civil rights targets behind when we moved out of the south, and desegregation was no longer the issue; the real question was whether we as black citizens would be allowed to play a full part in American society. And if America said no, it wasn't going to open the door to us, we had to be strong enough to kick it down.

I wished I could dedicate all my time to the movement but I had professional obligations – like touring Europe – to fulfil, and they isolated me. When I went on marches or played benefits I watched all the full-time activists embracing and laughing, grooving together, and I knew that when it was over they'd go home to eat, argue politics, listen to music, make love and sleep. The next day they'd make plans to meet up again on the next march and then go back into their communities to live out the ideas they believed in. They belonged; I didn't. I believed in the same things and fought the same fight, but there was no way I could know such closeness and community. On stage I might create a feeling of unity strong enough to keep me awake for a week, but I always came down to the knowledge that I was different. I had no community at the back of me, I was a national star and my job was to go wherever I was needed. I had no home town waiting, no Atlanta or Chicago to run to when I needed to recharge my batteries. When I took a break it was to headline a European jazz festival or play a weekend at the Hollywood Bowl – not the best places for plugging in to some downhome brotherhood.

I was rich and famous but I wasn't free. Most of the decisions I made were taken in consultation with my manager/husband, accountant, lawyer and record company. Like it or not, I couldn't do what I wanted and think about the consequences later; I had to plan months, sometimes years, ahead. So I felt part of the struggle, yet separated from it. I was lonely in the movement like I had been lonely everywhere else. Sometimes I think the whole of my life has been a search to find the one place I truly belong.

The only person who understood this was Daddy. My uncle in Philadelphia was politically active and told him what I was doing. We didn't talk politics much but every so often he told me how proud he was, usually at the exact moment a daughter needed to hear that from her father. But Daddy's main concern was me, not politics. He knew one day protest songs wouldn't be enough and I'd strike out down another road – he told me that once. The type of songs I sang made no difference to him, they were all part of what I was choosing to do; and whichever direction I chose was fine by him just so long as it helped me find peace of mind.

In June the riots started again, in Tampa, Cincinnati, and Buffalo, where fourteen rioters were wounded by police. I played the Newport Jazz Festival in July and got back to Mount Vernon to hear that thirty-six rioters had been killed in Detroit. The next day one of my friends in SNCC, Rap Brown, was shot and wounded in Maryland. News came through every day of friends getting arrested, beaten and intimidated. But there was no time to try and help because I had to prepare for another trip to Europe, followed by a week in Las Vegas. That was a joke – playing a city almost entirely segregated and stuffed full of gamblers and whores. I lasted four days in Vegas, at Caesar's Palace, then walked out.

My state of mind was fragile at this time. There were no more weird Cosby-tour episodes, but when I was very tired my subconscious took over and I'd go on auto-pilot until my mind was rested enough to turn itself back on. It was a relief when that happened: sometimes it made me relaxed and talkative, other times I cried for hours, letting the tension drip out of me. I was on the edge of exhaustion the whole time, two minutes away from collapsing. I gave up driving from fear of falling asleep at the wheel. Yet when the nights came around I'd lie awake until sunrise, crying – praying – for rest.

On those nights when nothing else worked, I'd reach for a drink. Andy tried to keep a lid on that, but I felt he was partly to blame anyhow. That blackboard still stood in our kitchen, and Andy was booking me on as many dates as ever. When I asked him to ease off he'd explain how I had to keep building my career, how it was too soon to relax. But I saw no reason why I couldn't do half the concerts for twice the money – no reason except Andy. He aimed too low, settled for too little and worked me like a carthorse, one-night show after one-night show.

Meantime the leaders of twenty black organizations met secretly in Washington and formed the Black United Front. After the last wave of riots we had to organize to defend ourselves against the backlash that would surely come. I played Carnegie Hall again in February and then went away to work on my next album. Six weeks later I drove to Westbury, Long Island, to prepare for a show. I arrived at the rehearsal room and found guys standing around stunned or huddled over the TV in the corner. It was 4 April 1968, and Dr Martin Luther King Junior had been murdered in Memphis.

Fresh rioting started almost immediately and the next day thirty-eight protestors died or were murdered. Twenty thousand people were arrested.

It was like the early days in the south all over again – full jails and no one with any idea what to do about it. For a while people walked around in a kind of daze and I wept along with them, but I couldn't understand why they were surprised by Martin's assassination: we'd already lost Malcolm, Medgar Evers, Emmett Till and hundreds, thousands of others down through our history. What happened on 4 April was no freak tragedy, it was the traditional white American tactic for getting rid of the black leaders it couldn't suppress in any other way. A desperate act by a country with nowhere to hide any more. Stupid, too, because the thing that died along with Martin in Memphis that day was non-violence, we all knew that. It was a time for bitterness – almost funny if it hadn't been so sad.

The president, LBJ, went on TV to declare 7 April a Day of National Mourning. This was the same man who had ordered thousands of US citizens – black and white – overseas to die in a foreign jungle while he ignored the war at home. Our president was obviously a man of violence. Why shouldn't the rest of us be the same?

My Westbury concert went ahead as scheduled on the 7th, the Day of Mourning. I performed 'Why? The King of Love is Dead,' a song in memory of Martin, for the first time that night. We recorded the set and included it on my 'Nuff Said!' album, which was Emmy nominated. I think my performance that night was one of my very best, focused by the love and quiet despair we all felt at our loss.

Meanwhile, in a Louisiana courtroom, Rap Brown was convicted on Federal firearms charges and freed pending appeal. He jumped bail and went underground. Years later Rap's appeal was granted after it was confirmed that the judge trying the case had been heard to say 'I'm gonna get that nigger' in open court. A snapshot of the times: martyred leaders and racist judges. American justice for the black man.

I left for Europe still grieving over Martin and we landed in Amsterdam to find the newspapers splashed with the details of Bobby Kennedy's assassination. It felt like the shutters were coming down on anyone who dared to suggest there was something seriously wrong with the state of our country. Stokely could hardly live for the harassment he was under – banned from travelling, in and out of jail, under FBI surveillance – and it was the same for Huey, Rap Brown, and many, many others. All over the country Panthers were being drawn into firefights with the police and then getting shot or burned to death. Those not already dead were exiled, jailed or underground.

But the show must go on. I played a night in Amsterdam, one in Rotterdam and then flew on to Montreux to play the Jazz Festival. As I walked out on stage the true weight of the last month's events hit me. I tried to gather myself – remembering Miz Mazzy, 'Composure Eunice, composure!' – but it didn't work. I sat down at the keyboard and tears started rolling down my cheeks, one after the other, unstoppable. The audience went quiet and people came over to see what was wrong, whether I was okay. Stupid, stupid questions. I was still crying ten minutes later when Andy helped me off. They happened to be filming the show that night. No one had the simple decency to turn off the cameras when they saw what was happening.

I wanted to cancel the tour and go home but Andy persuaded me to carry on, saying it would be a disaster if we stopped because after years of hit albums in Europe I finally had another hit single with 'Ain't Got No . . . I Got Life', a song from *Hair*, and we had to take advantage of the situation. It was a good point, made stronger by the fact that in Europe other people had been having hits for years using songs I first recorded: 'Please Don't Let Me Be Misunderstood' hit for The Animals, 'I Don't Want Him' for Nancy Wilson, 'I Put a Spell on You' for Alan Price, and 'The Other Woman' for Shirley Bassey. This list started to get me down after a while, especially when some of my audiences thought I played those songs because they were familiar crowd-pleasers, as if I only covered other artists' hits like some second-rate cabaret singer.

Now by a twist of fate I had a big hit with a cover version and the aim of our European tour was to exploit it. Andy wouldn't contemplate cancelling. He assumed he could talk me into carrying on – he was right in that – but he didn't realize, and I guess I didn't either, that his refusal to slow things down was becoming a big problem between us. We weren't communicating any more, and he was making decisions as my manager rather than as my husband. Maybe I should have stood up to him and made him understand, but I was too scared of what he might do. I remembered the time before we were married and kept my mouth shut.

Lack of communication was just one of our problems. Distracted by everything else going on, we'd let our relationship slide to the point where we never talked about our feelings or ambitions any more. They only got mentioned during the endless arguments we had – arguments which never settled anything. The tensions outside of the two of us, the pressures I felt from the movement, slopped over into our marriage and neither of us had the energy to clear them out. After Montreux we went on as before, touring, arguing and making up, never once getting close to the real issues. We just pushed on blindly until every so often my nervous exhaustion would force a crisis and I'd be late on stage, or give a bad performance. Then we'd rest up just long enough for me to recover before starting up again.

I guess I wanted more from Andy than he was prepared to give. Through our marriage and business arrangements Andy was wrapped around me like a snake, and there was no part of what I did that he didn't know about or influence. At first I liked it that way, because he took on many of the responsibilities, but eventually it began to suffocate me. I knew it was hard on Andy as well, and much of the strain between us came from simply working together too hard for too long, but the other areas of our marriage – which might have made our working life worthwhile – provided no comfort either. There was no passion between us: Andy said I was his 'sleeping pill' and that was how he used me at night, as a way of winding down. It wasn't enough for me. I'd known what good loving was like and I wasn't getting it any more, so my frustration grew.

What I needed most was something that few men I have ever known have been able to give me, a sense of peace. My whole life had been full of doubt and insecurity, and I was never confident about what I was doing. I'd lie awake nights worrying about complicated musical arrangements, whether or not we'd make the plane the next morning, if I was still attractive to men, anything and everything. All I really needed was someone to pull on my hand and say, 'You're okay, Nina. Leave yourself alone.' Andy wasn't the sort of man to do that, never had been.

I wrote a song, 'Four Women', which went into these feelings a little. The women in the song are black, but their skin tones range from light to dark and their ideas of beauty and their own importance are deeply influenced by that. All the song did was to tell what entered the minds of most black women in America when they thought about them-selves: their complexions, their hair – straight, kinky, natural, which? – and what other women thought of them. Black women didn't know what the hell they wanted because they were defined by things they didn't control, and until they had the confidence to define themselves they'd be stuck in the same mess forever – that was the point the song made. When 'Four Women' was released in 1966 some black radio stations banned DJs from playing it because they said it 'insulted' black women. It didn't, and banning it was a stupid thing to do, but I wasn't surprised. The song told a truth that many people in the USA – especially black men – simply weren't ready to acknowlege at that time.

It wasn't something I sang about a lot because the black struggle was my priority, but I knew if I tried I could compose a love song to take the scab off the terrible sore to do with the relationship between black men and women. Many of the women I knew were thinking the same way, that along with everything else there had to be changes in the way we saw ourselves and in how men saw us. At the same time I never thought of myself as part of women's liberation because I felt my needs were the same as any woman's, and the questions that female radicals were asking had no relevance to me. But although I needed the security of my marriage to Andy – I needed to be a strong man's wife – I guess deep down I fought against it. So I never sat down and tried to explain myself to Andy because, apart from the fact that he wouldn't listen, I was never aware of why I was so dissatisfied. I said I was tired of working and needed to rest, but the truth was I was tired of a hell of a lot more. And the more unhappy I got, the more tired I became.

I didn't suddenly wake up one morning feeling dissatisfied. These feelings just became more and more intense, until by the time the sixties ended I'd look in the mirror and see two faces, knowing that on the one hand I loved being black and being a woman, and that on the other it was my colour and sex which had fucked me up in the first place.

When I looked outside to my friends and their dreams I found no consolation. SNCC was dead in the water, with its most talented members exiled or imprisoned and the rest arguing among themselves. CORE was going the same way. The SCLC was still trying to recover after losing Martin. The anti-war movement had distracted most of the white liberal support we had left. Every black political organization of importance had been infiltrated by the FBI. Police terrorized our communities. Many people refused to admit it, but the plain truth was we were in retreat. In the movement the great plans for a national reawakening were being replaced by local projects in individual cities. The attitude was no longer 'What do we want?' but 'What can we get?'

The days when revolution really had seemed possible were gone forever. I watched the survivors run for cover in community and academic programmes and felt betrayed, partly by our own leaders but mostly by white America. And I felt disgusted by my own innocence. I had presumed we could change the world and had run down a dead-end street leaving my career, child and husband way behind, neglected. Optimists talked about the advances we had made, but all I saw were lost opportunities. In March 1970 I played a concert in Newark, New Jersey, in front of a segregated audience – entirely black – and I was full of hate, tearing spitefully into political leaders of all races. Backstage after the show people said I was an inspiration to continue the struggle, but that was the end of it all for me – the beginning of my withdrawal from political performance.

The old arguments with Andy started up again. As I had decided

In concert in Germany in 1970

At a reception in London in 1968 (Syndication International) (BELOW)

With Lisa, aged 9, in 1971 (Essence, Kowken Pakchanian) (RIGHT)

Meeting Greer Garson with Andy backstage at the Carnegie Hall in 1974 (BELOW)

With Big Mama Thornton (left) and Memphis Slim (right) in Montreal, Canada in 1979 (OPPOSITE, ABOVE)

With Stokely Carmichael, now Kwami Touré, and his wife at a picnic in Washington in 1981 (OPPOSITE, BELOW)

My mother, aged 83, in 1985 (ABOVE LEFT)

Lisa after joining the US Army in 1987 (ABOVE RIGHT)

At a concert in Boston with Freddie Hubbard in 1987 (Herb Snitzer) (OPPOSITE, ABOVE)

On board the Intrepid *in Rotterdam with a fan in 1988* (OPPOSITE, BELOW)

With Roland Grivel, my tour manager, Tipoteh from Liberia and Bob Dylan at a concert in The Hague in 1989 (Christina Suane) (ABOVE)

Visiting Pete Townshend in 1989 (BELOW)

At the Olympia in Paris with Chris White, Al Schackman, Paul Robinson, and Leopoldo Fleming in 1990 (ABOVE)

Enjoying life back at the top, 1991 (Sherry Barnett)

to be less involved in political performance it seemed a good time to ease off all round – a natural break. Andy didn't think so, and we argued on the way to the Newport Jazz Festival and on the way back home. As usual he refused to accept that I needed rest, and I realized he wasn't even sure I meant it. That did it. After all those years of arguing, persuading and begging, he didn't even believe I was serious about taking time off.

Lisa was staying with Andy's mother, and I realized that for once I could take the opportunity to do whatever I wanted without having to think of anyone else. So I walked out on Andy. I left my wedding ring on the bedroom dressing table and caught a plane to Barbados. It was the only thing I could do.

Barbados was heaven: I stayed at a hotel called Sam Lord's Castle and dedicated my life to becoming a beach bum. I swam, sunbathed, snorkelled and took scuba-diving lessons. At night I slept eight or nine hours straight through for the first time in years. I wallowed in everyday life like a prisoner released from Death Row, relishing each waking moment. I mastered scuba-diving and spent half of each day teasing sea anemones by stroking their little tentacles, chasing fish around the reef, and collecting conch shells for the guys in the kitchen to make me conch soup and sea-egg omelettes. It was the first holiday I'd had for seven years, and the first time I'd been alone for more than a few hours for as far back as I could remember. I wanted never to leave. I was in paradise and America didn't exist, had never existed . . . .

I knew Andy could find out where I was but I heard nothing from him. That didn't concern me; I wasn't going to think about anything except getting mind and body together. I figured we'd both benefit from a period of separation and get together again to sort things out when the time came.

Leaving Andy wasn't calculated: it was an act of desperation to show him I was serious about needing rest and that, if he wouldn't give it to me, then, hell, I'd take it anyway. I hadn't said our marriage was over or I was leaving him for good, because I hadn't spoken to him at all, I just left one day before he got home. Leaving my ring on the dressing table didn't mean I thought it was all over between us – I simply needed a vacation from my marriage for a while.

I was booked to play San Francisco at the end of September and figured Andy would call some time before we were due to leave, wanting to sort things out. When the date started to get close and there was no sign of him I assumed he was being proud – just like a man – and wanted me to make the first move. So I caught a plane back to New York. I got home to Mount Vernon and found the house dark, nobody home. Inside I looked around for signs of Andy but there weren't any – no clothes, no toiletries, none of the little things around the house that I knew he liked. No food in the refrigerator. Even the blackboard in the kitchen was gone.

It was our final communication breakdown. I'd left Andy in order to make a point about our marriage, and now he'd put up his hands and said, 'Okay, if that's the way you want it, I quit.' From the way he had moved out I knew he wasn't coming back. I turned off the lights, locked up the house and drove into the city to find a place to stay. Someone offered me an apartment and I took it. I wasn't ever going to live in that house again, not now. Everything to do with Mount Vernon was over.

I did the San Francisco concert and then flew back to Barbados. A couple of days later I was walking down to the beach when I tripped and fell awkwardly. I broke a bone in my foot and tore some knee ligaments. I was released from hospital after a few days and ordered to do nothing at all – just rest with my leg up. Sitting there immobilized, unable to swim or scuba, bored with reading magazines, I sat staring at the sea for hours, just thinking.

I was on my own again. Andy was gone and the movement had walked out on me too, leaving me like a seduced schoolgirl, lost.

I couldn't hole up in Barbados forever, and I knew I had to use this time to work out what I was going to do. My most straightforward problem was money. I wasn't poor, but most of what I had earned over the years was tied up in my publishing and production companies which Andy controlled. I talked to my brother Carrol in California, and he asked some hard questions about whether I knew how much there was, where the accounts were held and who controlled the assets. Andy had always been the one who took care of business and it frightened me how little I knew. While the situation with Andy was up in the air – in other words until we divorced – getting control of my financial affairs was difficult. I dealt with Andy through my lawyer, Max Cohen, but Andy wasn't being too forthcoming and there was talk of tax problems and controlled audits, royalty disputes and sub-publishing agreements. My head span with the details. All I really understood was that it was going to take a long, long time to sort out.

My concentration at this time wasn't too good, and one or two other matters distracted me when I should have been paying close attention. One of these distractions was a porter at the hotel, Paul, who became my lover. I met him on my very first day in Barbados when he showed me around the hotel complex. We got talking and he mentioned he had a motorcycle. When I told him I'd never ridden one he offered to take me on a ride straightaway, and he did, for miles and miles. Paul was a sweet guy and he had no idea who I was, which was important because it meant there were no hidden motives behind all the little kindnesses he showed to me. I was just a rich American lady as far as he was concerned, and when I told him I was famous he didn't believe me. Paul gave me all the attention and affection I'd been missing and I loved it – loved it! He took me riding on his motorcycle every day, took me to the movies, went swimming with me, everything – all the fun things I hadn't done for years. We had a short, uncomplicated affair which made me feel good about myself again. I liked Paul very much; in bed he was a tender lover and out of it he was kind and gentle, nice to be around.

No matter how much fun Paul was, I had to leave him behind and get back to the USA to try and sort out my affairs. After only a few weeks away things were beginning to pile up, and no sooner had I dealt with one problem than another two or three appeared. Apart from having to deal with Andy I had a series of concerts to play, musicians to organize and Lisa to take care of. At the same time I had to become familiar with areas of my work I knew nothing about, and I sat up at night reading about the legal and commercial sides of show business. The sub-publisher of my songs Ivan Mogull helped me, along with my old friend Max.

The problems started to become more serious. The Inland Revenue Service was starting to make enquiries about my income through the years I had been with Andy, but I didn't have access to my tax records because there had been a mysterious fire at our office and many of the documents they wanted had been destroyed. My record company was uneasy about my politics and took every opportunity to tell me so. The authorities in Mount Vernon began to harass me about the house – whether I was planning to live there again or sell it. There had been a flood which had caused severe damage on the ground floor and they wanted to know what was I going to about it. Then the IRS came back and said if I wasn't any more co-operative they might have to consider confiscating my property.

With the first concerts of my next tour only weeks away – and with them the chance to earn some badly needed money – priority one was getting a tour party together. Musicians were no problem, but I needed to find a road manager who would take the everyday strain while I concentrated on performing. It had to be someone I could trust. I had an idea: my baby brother Sam was a grown man now and a musician in his own right; he knew all about life on the road. I decided to go back home to Philadelphia to talk the idea through with him.

Of course when I got home there were a few other things that had to be cleared up first. When I told Momma that Andy and I had split she wasn't too concerned; broken marriages were what she expected from show business. Daddy didn't mind either – he'd never been too crazy about Andy. I didn't care what they thought anyway, distracted as I was by all my troubles and depressed by the realization that I would have to deal with them until the day I died (probably from exhaustion, no doubt on stage, most likely in front of TV cameras). Andy had left me – or I'd left him and then brought upon myself a terrible mess of debt, confusion and deception.

Those were hard and lonely days. As usual I had made a decision without thinking of the consequences and within months the structures that Andy and I had built together, which separated my professional and private lives, began to fall apart. I hadn't reckoned on the weight of responsibility I had to deal with once he'd gone. Now I understood how difficult it had been for Andy to get me to concentrate on things that weren't directly to do with the movement – like overseas tours or recording sessions booked weeks in advance, which we realized later coincided with important marches or campaigns. And until I started managing myself I never realized how skilful he had been, not just in organizing my itinerary but in saving me at least some private time – days when there was nothing to do but try and catch up on sleep, play with Lisa or go shopping. Simple, everyday things.

And it wasn't just that he managed to arrange dates so that I could escape from the pressures when I had to (I remembered cycling in London as if it was yesterday), it was the way he managed to keep performing, politics and our family life as separate ideas in my mind.

If I was depressed about performing I could be up about politics, which made performing more bearable. And vice versa. If both of those depressed me then I had Lisa – and Andy, damn him – as consolation, as something to cherish. But now, as I struggled on alone, everything fell into one pot and separate problems, separate depressions, mixed together into one big, black cloud.

I began to believe all my troubles were pieces of the same problem, which was that I had been betrayed. America had betrayed me, betrayed my people and stamped on our hopes. Andy had betrayed me too. And I felt let down by the black men who ran away from the showdown with white America: Andy, because he was a black man, became partly responsible for that too. I blamed all of my problems on these enemies and as I lost control, began to blame not just individuals but whole groups: Americans, the white man, men, record companies, promoters. I felt like I was being attacked on all sides: the whole world was ganging up on Nina Simone. So I turned to the people that should be there when you need them most, to my family. To Daddy. Then he betrayed me too, and I was lost.

All through my marriage I had been sending money to my parents; one of the first things Andy and I did as a married couple was arrange a monthly cheque for them, which increased every year. Daddy hadn't earned a regular wage since he stopped working at the dry-cleaning plant and the burden fell on Momma, who worked every hour she wasn't busy with the church. My folks had never been rich, and being able to help them made me feel wonderful. Of course it was my duty as a daughter to do it, but that wasn't the point. It was being able to make up for the sacrifices they had made for me which made me glow inside. Momma never made it easy for me to repay her, because she still felt uncomfortable with the life I led. So when I bought her a fur coat although, like any woman, she loved it, she didn't feel it was entirely right to take it, and I had to persuade her. And once she did accept it she wore it around the house more than outdoors because she didn't want the neighbours to think she was putting on airs. That was Momma, and while she made me want to tear my hair out sometimes at least she was consistent. Daddy wasn't so worried about accepting help, but that was because he needed it less. It was Momma who went out to work every day, tiring herself, doing what was needed to keep their home together.

So that was the situation when I was down in Philadelphia seeing

Sam and arranging the forthcoming tour with him, staying at my parents' home. One night Daddy and Sam were in the kitchen talking and I was on the phone in the other room. When my call finished I got up and started walking to the kitchen. I heard the sound of Daddy's voice, low and soft like he was telling a big secret, and I stopped in the passageway to try and listen. I strained my ears. Daddy was telling Sam how he had always been the one who provided the money in our family, how he had always made a good home for Momma and us children, how no one should forget that.

I stood there in the dark and listened to Daddy tell lie after lie after lie. It wasn't true, none of it, and even Sam, the baby, the youngest, had eyes and ears and a brain enough to know what Momma did and how she worked day after day. I stood there numb, unable to believe that Daddy would try to deceive Sam in this way. Daddy, who never lied about anything.

I had been misused and cheated all my life, and up to that point the one person I could rely on had been my father. The realization that he lied as well, like everybody else in the world, just crushed me. I felt the same disgust as when I heard the news of the Birmingham church bomb, and like then it was the final straw. I had spent years fighting for a lost cause; my marriage was over and my future was uncertain. After all the work I had done I didn't have financial security, and I couldn't even find out where most of the money I earned had gone. Of all the people I respected most had tricked and betrayed me – and now here was my father, who never lied, never, doing the same thing. If I had had a gun in my hand I might have killed him right there where he sat. As it was I walked into the kitchen and told him he wasn't my Daddy any more because I disowned him. From that moment I had no father. Then I walked out. Daddy didn't say a word.

I left for Europe almost immediately and toured through the spring of 1971. In between visits to New York to try and sort out my financial and legal problems I stayed in Barbados. Paul was around to indulge my taste for simple pleasures and every day on the island was a mercy, a way of keeping myself together. I tried not to think about Daddy. The rest of the family figured our split was something we'd have to sort out between us and didn't try to interfere.

For most of that year I just drifted along, trying to adjust to the changes in my life, separated from the things which had made me most secure. As Christmas approached I joined up with Jane Fonda and Donald Sutherland's 'Free the Army' tour, an anti-Vietnam revue which mixed music, comedy and protest. I just sang, keeping away from the politics. A couple of days after playing Philharmonic Hall in New York we moved out to Fort Dix, New Jersey, to play a free show for black GIs just back from the war. This concert was the one condition I insisted on before agreeing to join the FTA show, so that I could play at least once for my own people. The GIs – only kids, most of them – sat quietly and listened; the weariest, oldest audience I ever saw, lost in their own thoughts. They had only just got back from the war and were finding America difficult to cope with. Them and me both.

Back in Barbados I got a call from Lucille. She said Daddy was sick, and maybe I should come and see him. This was around fourteen months after we split, but my mind was set. I'd said I didn't have a father, and as far as I was concerned that was true whether he was sick or not.

Daddy got worse and my sisters Dorothy and Frances both called separately to say he was asking for me. He was in hospital in Shelby, a town near Forest City where Momma had been given her own church. I flew to North Carolina to be with my family but didn't go to see him.

Although everyone kept telling me Daddy's condition was worsening I refused to worry, convinced he would get better any minute. I stayed at home with Momma for as long as I could stand it and then moved down to Tryon to stay with Miz Mazzy. I had to get away from home because of the memories it brought back, and living in the white world, one step removed from the situation, was the only way I could endure it. I knew that if I'd have stayed at Momma's any longer I would have given in and gone to see him.

Daddy had cancer of the prostate and was wasting away. Every day Dorothy or Frances would tell me how much weight he was losing and how ill he looked. Over and over again he asked for me, and over and over again I refused him. Nobody understood why I wouldn't go to see him and I couldn't explain it so they'd understand. When I look back now on the way that I acted I know it sounds unforgiving and proud, but I wasn't cold and unemotional. I knew I was hurting Daddy and hurting myself more, but there was nothing I could do; I was helpless because of the vow I had made, the vow I had to obey.

Most of the time when you make yourself a promise and say, 'I'll never do that again,' it's unimportant and it doesn't matter if you break the promise the very next day, but this vow I had made not to see him was different and it clouded out everything else. I knew deep down Daddy knew I would have to keep to it; deep down he would understand.

It wasn't pride which kept me away. I was confused, unforgiving, and I never admitted the seriousness of Daddy's condition to myself, but I wasn't proud about what I was doing. I never thought, 'I'm right and that's all there is to it.' Never. While my family were at Daddy's bedside I was walking the streets of Tryon, reminding myself of the places we'd lived and the times we'd known, being with Daddy in a different way.

I was booked to play at the Kennedy Center in Washington in the second week of October. I couldn't cancel it because that would have been an admission that Daddy might die and I wasn't prepared to contemplate that. By the start of October the disease had reduced my father to less than ninety pounds. I moved back up to Forest City and tried to prepare myself for the Washington concert. The closer the day of the show came the weaker he got, and still he asked for me. The day before I was due to fly to the show Lucille came back from the hospital. She didn't have to say anything. My Daddy had died that afternoon.

I felt nothing, nothing at all. I wasn't cold or indifferent to his death; it was as if my ability to experience emotion had been cut out of me and I was dead inside. I left for Washington the next afternoon and as I flew they buried Daddy in Tryon in the graveyard on top of the hill behind the church. I wore black on stage that night and sang a new song, with words I had been writing right up to the moment he died:

I remember this afternoon
When my sister came into the room
She refused to say how my father was
But I knew he'd be dying soon.

And I was oh so glad, and it was oh so sad
That I realized that I despised this man I once called father.

In his hanging on, with fingers clutching
His body now just eighty-eight pounds
Blinded eyes still searching
For some distant dream that had faded away at the seams.
Dying alone, naturally.

I was his favourite child, I had him a little while
Just as long as I could play the piano and smile a little smile.
Just when I needed him most, he was already a ghost
And for all my life there were promises and they always have been
    broken.

Leaving me alone with all my troubles
Not ever once touching me and saying
'Daughter, I'll help you get over.'
Now he's fading away and I'm so glad to say,
He's dying at last. Naturally.

It's a very sad thing to see that my mother with all her heart
Believes the words that the Bible said 'Til death do us two part.'
For her that was forever and ay, he deceived her night and day
How could some English words so small affect someone so
    strangely?

Taking her away from us, her soul included
She might as well be gone with him, all the children are excluded.
Loneliness is hell, I know so well,
For I'm alone. Naturally.

I waited three weeks for him to die
I waited three weeks for him to die
Every night he was calling on me
I wouldn't go to him.
I waited three weeks for him to die
Three weeks for him to die.

And after he died, after he died
Every night I went out, every night I had a fight.
It didn't matter who it was with
'Cos I knew what it was about.

And if you could read between lines, my Dad and I close as flies.
I loved him then and I loved him still, that's why my heart's so
broken.

Leaving me to doubt God in His Mercy
And if He really does exist then why does He desert me?
When he passed away I smoked and drank all day,
Alone. Again. Naturally.

I knew nothing about death – that was the curse on me. I never
thought I wouldn't see him again. The idea that I couldn't go back to
Tryon to see Daddy didn't hit me for a long, long time, and my
realization that he was really gone, gone forever, was years and years
away. I didn't think of him as gone, and so the split between us lasted
right up to his death and beyond.

A week later Lucille was buried in the plot next to my father, struck
down by cancer. Nobody had known how very ill Lucille had been as
Daddy wasted away. We knew she was sick and that the doctors had
found a lump in her breast, but it didn't seem serious, at least not to
the family because Lucille had said nothing about it and to look at her
you'd have said she was as strong as ever. That was Lucille through
and through, fighting her own battles in her own way, alone. She
hadn't told anybody. Maybe she thought she could stare death in the
face and frighten him away, like she could anyone else.

I turned to stone inside. Lucille, who'd stepped into Momma's shoes
and taught me to be a woman, was gone. I tried to cry, I wanted to,
but tears wouldn't come. What sort of a person was I when sometimes
I could cry for hours without knowing why and yet couldn't find a
tear for Daddy and my beloved Lucille? What sort of person could
break down and cry on stage in Europe over the deaths of political
leaders and then refuse to visit her father's grave? What sort of person
could do this? What had happened to make me this way?

I had no answer to my own questions. I fled to Barbados pursued
by ghosts: Daddy, Lucille, the movement, Martin, Malcolm, my
marriage, my hopes.

Chapter 9

Barbados – as usual – tried to convince me that nothing beyond the horizon existed, but this time it didn't work. I had so much to grieve for I didn't know how to begin, and on those rare days when I did start to come out of my dark mood strange little coincidences pushed me back down. This was the time when I heard 'My Happiness' on the radio and those memories of Edney came back in a rush. The tears fell like rain and they wouldn't stop, there was so much to cry for. But the sun still rose in the morning, to set at night, and after a while I was able to seal my unhappiness up inside me, in some bleak and private place. I tried to live a normal life again – during the daytime at least. The real pain came at night, surging out of the dark instead of sleep.

Lisa was with me and we spent good times together, the sort of time she hadn't had too much of while I was out on the road with Andy. Empty afternoons were filled by Paul, his motorbike and his undemanding loving. I thought I had all I wanted, at least until I felt strong enough to go back out into the world again. But although neither of us knew it as we rode his motorcycle along the island's back roads, Paul was doomed. It was a funny thing, the way Paul thought we were forever and then made certain we weren't by introducing me – indirectly – to his successor. It all started one time when Paul was acting high and mighty and I said something like. 'You can't say that to me, don't you know who I am?' Paul laughed and said 'No,' like he usually did when I asked that question. I decided to show him exactly how famous I was so I went over to the hotel and demanded to know who the most important person in Barbados was, and where he lived. They told me a certain Mr Earl Barrow was the Prime Minister and he lived on the other side of the island. I got directions, put Lisa in the car and set out to find him.

My plan was to introduce myself to the most important man in Barbados, may be have dinner with him, say nothing to Paul and wait until he read about it in the newspaper. Then I'd smile sweetly and say: 'The Prime Minister? Oh, didn't I tell you? He's a good friend of mine.' There were quite a few cars parked in the driveway of the PM's residence when I arrived, because he had called a press conference to talk about some local political issue. I had taken the time to dress properly for my introduction to the man and Lisa looked gorgeous too, her hair full of coloured bands. We strolled into the conference room to say hello, looking real good. All the press knew who I was and the cameras started clicking, flashbulbs going crazy, and within two minutes they had a front-page story. And I didn't have to ask 'Hey, which one of you guys is the Prime Minister?' either, because at the end of the room a distinguished-looking, dark-skinned man stood up and walked over to greet me. His hair was greying and he was a little stout, but he had the attitude that goes with being the top man. Handsome, too, I noted. When he spoke his voice was quiet, and he expected to be listened to. But I looked into his eyes and could tell right away he was shy, for all that.

He welcomed me to the island, said he'd heard I was visiting, and asked me where I was staying. I told him, and he immediately invited me to come and live at Kampala, on the PM's personal estate, in one of the houses on the beach.

I didn't know what to say to this offer at first but his personal physician, Dr Esther Archer, was standing nearby and she joined in too, saying sure I should come, I'd love it. So I did, and we moved in that night. My new house was on the beach at Paradise Island: it had three bedrooms, a big kitchen, big lounge and big dining room, and a garage with its own car. Servants to care for Lisa and me. Paradise Island all right. Surf rolled up outside my bedroom window, just beyond the swimming pool.

Poor Paul. He didn't know it but he'd pushed me into the path of a guy who came close to matching my blueprint for the ideal man. Earl Barrow was strong, political, well mannered, rich and secure enough to accept me as both woman and star. When I looked into his eyes that first time I knew he wanted me too, which was the fairy on the Christmas tree. He dropped by late that first night to see how I had settled in, and we sipped drinks and chatted by the pool. He came along the next night, and the one after that, and soon his visits became a nightly ritual I looked forward to. In his own reserved way the PM was courting me, and I was thrilled. I dropped Paul as gently as I could.

I knew the PM was married because I'd met his wife Caroline in the beauty salon at the Hilton Hotel one time. She was American too, from New Jersey. Pretty with it, but I didn't worry about her – not after the first few visits the PM made. He worked very long hours, so when he came to me at night it was always late – rarely before 1 a.m. – and he stayed until four, when he went home to his wife and then back to work by nine the next morning. I'd spent my days swimming, scuba-diving, playing with Lisa, and then waited up for him. When he arrived I'd cook him something simple to eat – simple because he got so much rich food at official banquets. He'd come in dog tired, lay his head on my shoulder and say, 'Oh, Nina, I'm so tired of this food they serve me all the time. It's champagne, it's fancy dinners. I just want some ordinary food like my servants give me. Do you have a piece of bread and butter?' I'd give him the bread and butter and he'd fall asleep on my shoulder holding it in his hand.

On nights when he wasn't too tired we made love, and he was as careful and courteous in bed as out of it. He made me wish for more carefree abandon sometimes, but the man didn't have it in him – he was so dedicated and considerate. I didn't mind being his mistress; the novelty excited me, and if you're the mistress of a PM it's a luxurious position, decadent almost. I was his courtesan and he my pasha.

We had to be discreet, but every now and then I managed to pull him out of his shell. We went out driving in a jeep one afternoon and I was trying to get him to say he loved me. He was teasing, refusing to say it, so when he stopped I jumped out, stripped and ran naked into the field by the side of the road, shouting 'You don't want me! He chased out after me, laughing. Caught me, too. At home that night he cooked Chinese food and serenaded me, singing 'The Folks who Live on the Hill'. We both had what we wanted at that moment – an easy fun relationship with no particular future in mind, just the present to enjoy.

Once that was understood, I got to enjoy all the trappings of my position. When I returned to Barbados after a concert tour I walked off the plane into an official limousine waiting for me on the tarmac. No customs, no passport stamp, nothing. When I got bored with one official residence I moved into another, and when that

131

bored me I moved again.

The only problem with living in the PM's houses was he always had keys and could walk in any time. He never understood why that worried me, and one afternoon it created a wonderful misunderstanding. Al Schackman came down to stay just after I'd moved into a new place, and I told him I'd like the locks changed. I didn't say why, I just said I felt unsafe, so Al fitted a new lock. The PM came round the next afternoon while I was in town arranging for my Steinway to be shipped from New York. Al had been taking a swim and came back up to the house to find a man he'd never seen before trying the lock on the door. Al got into his uptown real quick and shouted, 'Hey buddy, what're you doin'?' The stranger just looked at him and so Al asked again.

'Where's the lady?' was the only reply he got.

'She's out just now but I'm her friend,' said Al.

'When shall she return?' said the stranger.

Al lost his patience and started to ask what the heck this guy thought he was doing trying to open the door to somebody else's house, and anyway didn't he know the locks had been changed?

The man just stood there and said, 'Oh, I see.' Then he turned and started walking away.

All the way through their conversation the guy's cut-glass English accent had annoyed Al, so as the man walked off Al asked, 'And who shall I say called?' in a sarcastic kind of way. The stranger stopped: 'The Prime Minister.' Al looked along the driveway, saw the official limousine and thought, 'Oh shit . . .' I got home half an hour later and Al told me the whole story. We rolled on the floor, screaming.

That wasn't quite the end of it. Two nights later I was invited to a big party at the PM's official residence and I took Al along. The PM was standing in a white tuxedo welcoming his guests. We got to the front of the line and I said, 'Mr Prime Minister, I would like you to meet my old and trusted friend and guitarist Al Schackman.' The two of them looked at each other, each remembering the last time they'd met. The PM put out his hand and said, 'Ah, Mr Schackman. How do you do?' He never cracked a smile. The incident was never mentioned again, not once, even though Al and the PM met often after that first encounter.

Sometimes, half-serious, I asked the PM when we'd get married. He always said 'I'm already married', and I always replied, 'Well, divorce your wife.' The truth was that divorce would mean the end of Earl Barrow's political career, and he was a politician first to last. The more I got to know him the more I realized he loved his country and the responsibility of his job, and he'd never let it go willingly. We'd go swimming together and he'd lie on the beach and say, 'This is my island, this is where I belong.' He couldn't imagine living anywhere else.

One afternoon he got up to leave early because he had to open a new factory. I wanted him to stay and said I didn't see why a PM should lower himself to work like that. 'But it's part of my job to do it,' he said, 'it's part of my job to do anything which helps the people of this island.' He meant it. He was probably the first honest politician I'd met who actually held office. Nothing was too menial, none were too high or low for him to visit, and when I spent time in public with him I saw how much he was loved. I could see this man was rooted, secure where he was and happy to be there. I couldn't give him anywhere near the same amount of pleasure he got from being PM – no woman could – and his attitude to me was that he liked me around but if I went, well, I went; he'd still have his island. I respected that because I was used to a similar kind of double loyalty, to my lover and to my talent. Anyone who marries me marries my talent as well, and that's not the same thing as marrying the woman: the woman might want to stay with her man, but when Nina Simone the singer, the artist, has other things to do, the needs of the woman most often come second. So it was for Earl Barrow, the Prime Minister and the man.

Our affair ended quite suddenly. One small incident seemed to bring us crashing down, but I realized later that the PM had decided to end it all for political reasons, before things got out of hand, and he was looking for an excuse. We started to fall apart fourteen months after we first met: I was over in New York in my apartment in the ASCAP building and the PM was in town staying with me for a couple of days. We had a wonderful time, and after he left I decided to move everything I had to Barbados so I could be near him permanently: piano, furniture, rugs, everything. I didn't tell the PM what I was doing. I also didn't know about the various official hoops you have to jump through if you want to become a resident of Barbados. As a result my belongings were stopped at the airport.

All of a sudden it made no difference how friendly I was with the

PM. At the time I was too dumb to understand what his indifference signified – too optimistic, too deluded. I was a classic mistress from first to last and I made the classic mistake: I assumed it would be better to be his wife. I knew it would be difficult – in reality it was imposssible – but I convinced myself all the problems could be overcome. The attraction, of course, was the security that life as the PM's wife offered: roots, prestige and a different, undemanding, fame. My things went into storage while I tried to sort out a resident's bond and I moved into a new official house, Oldtrees, near Sam Lord's Castle. The PM didn't come to see me as often as before but I told myself he was a busy man and it didn't mean anything. It did, of course: he was trying to let me down gently. I started filling in the night hours he used to devour, seeing friends when he wasn't around.

For some time I had been pestering him to fly me in his official jet to Martinique for lunch. He kept promising and putting it off and promising again, until one afternoon he sent a message that we were going the next morning. That night I went out dancing and came home at 5 a.m. At seven, a driver knocked on the door to take me to the airport. I told him I was sorry but I was too tired, and could he please excuse me to the PM?

It was a thoughtless thing to do, and I never stopped to think how difficult it must have been for the PM to arrange the trip. He didn't say anything about it, but he never forgave me. A few weeks later I was asked to leave Oldtrees by a government official; Lisa and I moved to a cottage in the grounds of Sam Lord's Castle – the hotel I had first stayed in when I came to Barbados. Two days later we were robbed there, by a masked man. He wanted to rape my daughter as well, but I frightened him away. When I told all these things to the PM he was sympathetic, but didn't do anything about it. He just said he was running for re-election so he had to be more careful now, and anyway he didn't have any time to spare on special investigations. Although the message was obvious enough I didn't see it even then, and assumed that once the election was over we would go back to the way we were. In the meantime I thought it would be a good idea to leave Barbados for a while, so Lisa and I flew to New York.

I had kept an apartment in New York ever since I'd left Mount Vernon; much as I wished I could keep away from America, I was drawn back for a variety of unpleasant reasons. I divorced within a year of Andy walking out of the Mount Vernon house: I flew to Santo

Domingo with Max Cohen and arranged it through the courts there. Two days later I flew back to the USA a single woman again. The business side of our relationship had not been sorted out yet, but I couldn't wait any longer – I wanted a definite break, legal and binding. It was a big mistake. I should have hired the best divorce lawyer in town to sort out every side of our affairs and then divorced him, but I couldn't wait, I wanted out too bad. So we divorced as two people and ignored the companies, monies owing and debts which hung over the Nina Simone organization at that time. I pressed ahead blindly, ignoring questions like which of us was responsible for the missing tax returns that the IRS were getting so excited about. I knew the IRS meant trouble but the thought of dragging our divorce out over years, arguing over everything, was too much to bear. Our marriage was over and I didn't want to spend any longer than I had to raking through the ashes.

Once the divorce was finalized I tried to make some sense of my affairs but the truth was for all those nights spent studying the business I couldn't do it. Not because I was dumb, but because I was in America. When I stepped off the plane from Barbados I looked around and everything reminded me of Daddy and Lucille. The America I'd dreamed of through the sixties seemed a bad joke now, with Nixon in the White House and the black revolution replaced by disco. I came to expect despair every time I set foot in my own country, and I was never disappointed. I longed to escape, and so when problems came up which needed weeks of close attention I lost all hope of ever solving them and cut out back to my island, trying to forget, hoping – hoping, after all I'd seen – for the best. With Daddy and Lucille gone and Momma deep into her church the heart was ripped out of my family. I had done things I couldn't explain to the people I loved most: Daddy, Momma, my sisters. I couldn't go home without explaining myself, and I didn't know how. The truth was I had no home any more.

I was lost and I struck out at the people around me, which destroyed my recording career in America. The protest years were over not just for me but for a whole generation and in music, just like in politics, many of the greatest talents were dead or in exile and their place was filled by third-rate imitators. All record companies prefer third-rate talents to true genius because they can push them around more easily, make them change their clothes or politics just to sell more records.

My record deals expired along with my marriage and I became one more black artist 'difficult to place' in the neat world the labels created. For black musicians the result of the sixties was exile to dance music and the old black ghettoes of jazz and blues. The only black artists that record companies liked were those who crossed over by playing music for the white mass market, music which ran scared of its own colour. What had happened to great black record labels like Motown, Stax and Atlantic? Where was James Brown in the mass market? Where was Aretha Franklin? Where was Nina Simone? Nina Simone was walking away from an industry with no place for her, an industry which had been happy to sell millions of her records through the sixties and then turned around and said they didn't think people wanted to listen to those kind of records any more.

I thought about that on 11 May 1974 when 100,000 black people turned up to salute me in Washington DC when I was the guest of honour at the annual Human Kindness Day celebration. Mohammed Ali presented me with a citation at the Washington Monument grounds, and once the six-hour free concert that followed was over I was driven to the Smithsonian Institution for a dinner in my honour, with specially composed tributes and entertainment. I was proud to be saluted in this way by my own people, the people I cared most about, but it didn't change the way I felt about America. We knew, all of us veterans of the movement, what was going on all right. The establishment was biting back. It was no accident that the most active black musicians couldn't get recording deals with the major labels, no accident at all.

Momma was there to see me that day in Washington. They flew her in especially, and when we got out of the car at the Memorial grounds and thousands of fans pressed forward to catch a glimpse of Mohammed Ali and me I looked in her face and wanted to cry at the concern I saw there. I think it was the first time she ever understood what I had become, that I was important to thousands of people and they all wanted a part of me.

As they pushed forward she looked at them and then back at me and her eyes said, 'I don't care what you all want, this is my daughter. Leave her alone, she's mine.' I had wanted her there to find out if she would ever be proud of me, but I discovered instead that Momma wanted to protect me. She and I were of the same blood and anyone wanting to get me would have to go through her first. Our blood was a bond between us which rose above our differences to bind us together, and it always would. I had never realized that before and it was precious knowledge. I carry it with me always.

I came back from Human Kindness Day straight into a crisis over the house in Mount Vernon, which the local authority were insisting I did something about, because the building was falling into a state of disrepair and by law they could force me to sort it out one way or another. I was in Barbados when I heard, and this new pressure came at the same moment when the PM began to cut me out of his future. So I paid no attention to the problems with the house: I was a few hundred miles away with bigger issues at stake. When the IRS heard about the house they closed in too. I told Max Cohen to sort it out if he could, but there was nothing he could do. My house was confiscated and sold. In 1962 it had cost me $37,000; I got $1400 back from the sale – all that was left after the County and IRS had finished. I found this out the day I flew back from Barbados with Lisa, trying to convince myself everything would turn out fine with the PM. It confirmed what I already knew; every time I arrived in the USA something terrible happened.

Lisa and I arrived in New York with only the clothes in our suitcases because everything else was still in storage, impounded in Barbados. We sat in my apartment and looked at each other, a mother and her twelve-year-old daughter, wondering what to do next. If ever I needed a friend it was then, and I'd almost forgotten that I had such things until Miriam Makeba called. Through the years of our friendship I had sworn many times that I would go with her to Africa the next time she went, and just as often she'd sworn to take me. When I'd finished telling Miriam the miserable story of the past few months she said, 'Well, are you ready to come to Africa?' I remembered the crowds around the plane steps the day the AMSAC group arrived in Lagos, when I was happy and had only been married two weeks. Africa. The word ran around my head. Africa, half a world away from New York. Maybe I could find some peace there, or a husband. Maybe it would be like going home.

Miriam had been invited to Liberia to attend a gala rally celebrating President Tolbert's new government and she wanted me to go along. I knew a little about North Africa because I'd stayed in Morocco after one trip to Europe, but the AMSAC trip had been my only experience to date of West Africa – the heart of the old slave trade and the home of my ancestors before slavery, when they were free. Liberia had been founded by freed slaves returning to settle in Africa, and their descendants made up the most prosperous section of Liberian society – people like the Dennis family, the Parkers, the Brights, the Tubmans and the Tolberts, with the new president among them. Liberia and America were connected through history in a positive way, and Liberian culture and society reflected that. It was a good place to start at for any Afro-American looking to reconcile themselves to their own history.

But those weren't my thoughts as I prepared to leave America behind me once and for all. I was seduced by the Africa in my mind, my mythical home. My Africa had no countries, just hundreds of different peoples mixed through history into a rough cocktail and forced to seed an exiled nation in a far-off country: my great-grandfather, Grandma, Daddy, Momma, me.

Miriam understood my idea of Africa because she was 'Mother Africa', famous and loved throughout the continent and a friend of kings and princes, prime ministers and presidents. She was also smart enough to realize that modern Africa might overpower an innocent Afro-American like me, and so for my first step she chose Liberia, a place where I could relish the differences and yet still feel secure with the similarities.

Lisa and I hardly had anything to pack, so we just upped and went. We – the three of us, including Miriam – arrived in Monrovia on 12 September, Lisa's birthday. There was an official reception for us at the airport – Miriam got this treatment wherever she went in Africa but they knew all about my coming too – and we just had time to change and rest a little before we were driven to the Presidential Palace to be guests of honour at a special party. I met the president, vice-president and all the other cabinet members, shook hands with ambassadors and emissaries and drank champagne all night long. Everyone in Liberia knew who I was, and most of them had at least one or two of my records – I was flattered but not surprised, remembering that Miriam had first heard me on the radio in South Africa all those years ago. Liberians are naturally affectionate, open people, proud of their country, and the fact that a famous black American had decided to come home – which was what they called it – to stay, meant something special to them. It felt as if the whole country had turned out to celebrate my arrival; I was overwhelmed by hospitality. And no one suggested I play for them, not once in the whole time I was there, which turned out to be years. To them it was enough that I was there at all.

I woke up on my first morning in Liberia to find photographs of our arrival on the front pages of the newspapers. I had told some reporter it was my daughter's birthday, and we'd not finished breakfast before one of my new friends called to invite Lisa to a birthday party she'd arranged for her. They plaited her hair with coloured ribbons, sang her songs and gave her presents. The next day it was my turn again, a surprise party in the house on the beach which the President's daughter had given me to stay in for as long as I wanted. For a week I went to a different party every night and had to postpone invitations to others, pleading exhaustion.

I wouldn't have believed it before I arrived, but Liberia did feel like home and I loved everything about it. I loved the way it took two hours to drive the three miles into town during the rainy season, when the road down to the beach turned to mud and the rain beat so hard on the windscreen you couldn't see past the wipers. I loved the way it took me four hours to teach my cook, Nathaniel, how to make an omelette, and I loved the way Nathaniel had forgotten how to do it by the very next day. And I loved the parties, the fun, the palm wine. Liberia was a release; after all those years of being a wife, mother, activist and star all at the same time I was just a mother with her child happy in school and nobody looking over my shoulder telling me what to do.

They said I was wild. I wore nothing but a bikini and boots all day long and danced about with the weight gone from around my shoulders. Miriam knew how much I needed this time and she got busy the moment we arrived, fixing up six men for me, all wealthy and single, all prospective husbands. It was up to me to find out just how prospective.

My third night in Liberia I went out on my first date with one of these guys, a man named Clarence Parker – one of the big Parker family and therefore one of the most important men in the country. Rich, too – Miriam didn't give me no riff-raff – since he had fifteen thousand acres of oil-producing palm trees. I went over to his house and he took me into one room to show me his art collection. He said he was very proud of his paintings, very proud. I looked around the room and every picture showed people in different sexual positions:

up, down, around, you name it. Clarence poured me more champagne and asked me to choose my favourite – he made me laugh, he was so interested in my opinion. Then he said he was sure I had never really enjoyed sex in my life but added, 'Don't worry, Nina, I'm here to take care of that now!' I turned him down because these were early days, and I had five more men to check out before I got round to making those sorts of decisions.

When Clarence saw his art collection wasn't going to work he took me along to a nightclub instead, to a place called the The Maze. It was a small club that held about fifty people, but most of Liberian high society was there that night. By the time I got there I'd drunk a bottle and a half of champagne and was feeling just fine. I started dancing, and the champagne and my happiness and the music got to me all at once, got to me good. I started stripping my clothes off while I danced, and everybody started clapping, hooting, feeding me champagne. I got down to nothing at all and danced naked for at least two hours, having the time of my life. Later I wrote a song about it, 'Liberian Calypso'. I was so happy to be home, so happy to be in town at a place I could do this where everyone laughed and clapped rather than having me arrested.

When I woke up the next day – alone – I was myself again, and although I didn't regret my night for a moment I was scared because a friend called to tell me word had got around town and even the president was asking his friends if I was the woman 'who came from America and stripped off at The Maze?'. I thought the president might be shocked and order his police to deport me, a prospect I couldn't bear. My fear lasted until the next day, when I heard the president had gone to The Maze the night before hoping to catch a repeat performance! If I didn't know it already, that proved Liberia was my kind of country.

Within a few weeks I felt as if I had been living in my house on the beach all my life. Situated where it was, a little way outside of the town centre, its location was just far enough from Monrovia's noise and excitement to allow me peace and quiet whenever I wanted without being cut off. At parties and embassy receptions I mixed with the very top of Liberian society and at the beach I hung out with everyday people: so it was a nice mix and I felt I knew everybody. I was settled, but the ghosts in my memory hadn't disappeared – they were just bedded down deeper and tormented me less often. I still thought of Daddy sometimes, and when I did I became unhappy again, mainly because I didn't know what I thought about him, I was still so confused.

I had arrived in Liberia with no idea of how long I intended to stay; after a few hours I knew it was going to be a long, long time – forever, if everything worked out – and so I had to return to the USA to arrange for money to be sent to me and to pick up some of my things and let people know where I was. I put the trip off again and again but eventually I couldn't wait any longer, so I left Lisa in the care of the president's daughter and flew back to New York. I flinched at every noise, expecting the terrible events that always hit me when I arrived in the country that had disowned me. But this time nothing terrible happened except that I got depressed and longed for Liberia and my house on the beach. America was Daddy, and he got under my skin. I rushed around sorting out as much as possible until I couldn't stand it any longer and caught the first plane back to Liberia, back home.

It seemed like a normal flight, but it was the start of the amazing experience I mentioned when I was describing Daddy's sickness back in Tryon when I was a young girl, all that time ago. I had called Liberia to let them know I was coming, and when I got off the plane in Monrovia one of my best Liberian friends, Millie Buchanan, was waiting in the arrivals lounge. Millie took one look at me and said, 'I've got to take you somewhere right now.' I looked at her like she was crazy and asked her what she was talking about, but she wouldn't say anything more. She just bundled me and my luggage into her car and we drove off. We went to a part of the city I hadn't seen before and stopped outside a little house. Millie took me into the house and made a call, and a little while later an ordinary-looking man came to the door, dressed in a neat, grey suit.

He was a witch doctor. Before I lived in Liberia I thought African witch doctors dressed in bizarre clothes and carried skulls on sticks around with them, but that was just the result of ignorance and western prejudice against African medicine. I knew enough about Africa by now to understand there was nothing weird about tribal medicine or what it could do. But I was still puzzled about why I had been brought to see this man. Millie told me she had known there was something wrong as soon as I got off the plane but she couldn't tell what it was, so she'd called in an expert. The tribal doctor – this ordinary-looking man – took some small bones out of his jacket pocket and squatted down on the floor. He tossed them in the air and studied the pattern they made when they landed. He didn't say anything, just sucked on his teeth a little, then picked up the bones and threw them once more. Silence again.

Finally he looked up at me and spoke. He said: 'Who is this person on the other side who loves Carnation milk?' Daddy. I turned to stone. Carnation milk, a little sugar, vanilla, and a beaten egg, every day for months until the wound in his stomach healed and he could take solid food. I was four years old and I made it for him every day. He was talking about Daddy. He described how my father looked, tall and so thin, the clothes he wore. And other – private – details. Daddy, for certain.

The medicine man said: 'Whoever this man is, he's a doctor now and he can help you from the other side, but you must forgive him for something he did while he was here.' I just nodded, I couldn't speak. Then the man told me the ritual I had to obey in order to reconcile myself with my father. I had to stay in the house for three days without seeing or speaking to anybody; I had to put my hair in a wrap, not smoke or drink anything, and lie in bed with a tin of Carnation milk under my pillow for those three days. I had to pretend my father was sleeping in bed with me. If I obeyed the ritual everything between us would be forgiven and Daddy's spirit would be with me again. Once he was sure I understood all his instructions the witch doctor picked up his bones, shook my hand and left. Millie paid him some money and went away to look for a tin of milk. She found one, gave it to me and left.

I did exactly as I was told. I lay in bed picturing myself as a little girl and imagined Daddy there beside me, the two of us asleep in each other's arms, a child and her father. No one disturbed us – Millie made sure of that – and after three days I awoke and felt a weight leave me.

It was a distinct physical sensation, as if I had lost half my body weight in one sudden moment. And the next instant I saw my father: I am not allowed to say how, because the tribal doctor swore me to secrecy, but he was there in front of my eyes for a short while and then he left.

His spirit remained in the room with me and has stayed with me ever since. From that third morning to the present day my father's spirit has been watching over me, and when he knows I need to feel him near he comes around and makes sure I know he's there.

142

Sometimes when I'm worrying about an important decision and don't know which path to take he comes into the room and stays until I make my decision, and if it's the wrong one he won't leave until I change my mind. Only when I've decided correctly does he go.

In Africa spirituality isn't separated from everyday life like it is in the west and nobody laughed or thought my ritual was strange when I talked about it, or mentioned my father's spirit being around. I used to describe Daddy and I coming together again to anyone who was interested, but I stopped after some journalists wrote stories describing how I talked to walls and imagined Daddy's ghost sitting in the chair next to me. It wasn't like that at all, and I realized that if people weren't prepared to try and understand there was no point talking to them anyhow. What was true on the day I left that house in Liberia was that, for the first time since I had banished Daddy from my life, I could think of him without wanting to cry and without feeling that cutting pain.

By this time I had seen all of the six men Miriam lined up for me, and while they were all charming, rich and attentive none of them quite hit the spot. My naked dance at The Maze had convinced many of the men I knew that I was easy pickings, but in fact I was the exact opposite. Sure, I went out with men – dancing, or to dinner, let them escort me to parties – but that was it. It was enough for me to enjoy the mental release this beautiful country had given me, which included the easing of my pain over Daddy. I felt no need to complicate my life with pointless love affairs. On the other hand I hadn't given up on men – no way. I was just waiting for the right one to come along, a serious man. I was interested in a husband, someone to take care of me.

Miriam was making plans to fly down to Kinshasa to see Mohammed Ali fight there, the 'rumble in the jungle'. She invited me along, but now I was safely back in my house on the beach I wasn't going anywhere in a hurry. The day after she left I had a phone call from a girlfriend of mine, Doris Dennis, whose husband was a close relative of the foreign minister. I knew her husband well, and admired him. Doris wanted to know what I was doing at that very moment; I said I wasn't doing anything, so she told me come over. She said, 'Somebody wants to meet you, my father-in-law, and he makes his son look silly by comparison.' I went over but he wasn't there, he'd gone off leaving his card for me. On the back he'd written 'Don't move, I'll be back in an hour. In Africa men are the boss. We will be married in six weeks, C.C. Dennis.' I couldn't believe the nerve of the man to write me a card like that, but I was intrigued to meet him and so I waited. And an hour later he came in – or I should say he swept in, like a whirlwind. He was tall and handsome with grey hair, dressed in a suit. As he came into the room in one gesture he swept me off my feet, kissed me squarely on the lips and said, 'Doris, go get the silver cups!' She got them and he filled them with wine and we drank to our marriage in six weeks. I hadn't said a word – I couldn't think of anything to say to this man, he moved so fast. He put the cup down and said: 'You have been sent here to me. My wife put me out of her bed after our second son and I don't know why. I have to marry a younger woman.' He was 70 years old, and more exciting and attractive than any man I had ever met half his age.

C.C. had everything planned between us and he shouted it out to the world: 'I know that you must be tired – you've been waiting here for me for a couple of hours. So pack up your things in the morning and we'll go to my house in the mountains. We will spend four days, and in that time we'll see if you can get the old thing up.' He went on, 'If you can or not is up to you. It's time for you to go now.' I still hadn't said anything. C.C. looked at me, expecting me to do what he said and so I got up and his driver took me home.

Faced with a man like this, I had no choice; he was like a Liberian Rhett Butler. The next morning I sat waiting with my clothes packed into a little wine-coloured suitcase. As I sat there waiting, a woman called Martha Prout called in. When I had first arrived in Liberia they had made Martha my African momma, trusting her to look after me and help me along. She lived next door and was always around helping me out, taking care of Lisa when I went away sometimes, just like a real momma. Martha winked and said, 'I know where you're going. Are you going to live in the town or the country?' I said I didn't know what she was talking about.

Martha laughed. 'Yes you do, child. Everyone knows you're going to marry Mr Dennis. Well, let me see how you look.' I stood up while she checked me over. 'I approve,' she said, 'go on and have a good time.'

C.C.'s car arrived soon afterwards and we set out. He was talking a mile a minute as the car flew along, saying things like: 'I know you drink too much, but if you stop drinking for three days I will reward you.' As I took this in he moved to another topic: 'I know your piano is in Barbados, but I will send for it. I know you're used to money so I'll give you $25,000 a year of your own and you can do what you please with it.' The drive to his estate took two or three hours, and C.C. had me entranced the whole way. There were thousands and thousands of rubber trees on both sides of the road and they all belonged to him. Finally we arrived at his house: C.C.'s mansion, and the centrepiece of his estate.

Sitting on the steps waiting for us was an old man, older than God. As our car drove up he hoisted up a flag on the pole in front of the house to tell all the estate workers C.C. was back. When C.C. got out this old man said to him, 'Master, I'm glad you're home.' This was all very strange to me and I felt uneasy. A plantation, and an old man who called the owner 'master'? It reminded me of the deep south too much – change the colour of C.C.'s skin, drop back 150 years and we could have been in Chesney County, South Carolina; the workers around the back of the house would have been my great-grandparents. What I didn't know, and what C.C. told me later, was that the old man used the term 'master' when addressing him because C.C. was a freemason.

Beyond the old man in the hallway of the house seventeen men were lined up to greet us – the household. We went inside and C.C. said, 'Old man, say the prayer.' The old man began to pray. He thanked God for the air, the sun, the water, his master, his guests, the estate workers, Miriam, everybody he could think of. I glanced at my watch; I'd never heard anyone pray so passionately for so long. After forty minutes he was still praying and I felt the tears coming down my cheeks. I didn't know why I was crying, but I couldn't stop.

Finally the prayer ended. Everybody clapped and C.C. said, 'Old man, that's the finest prayer you've ever given!' Then he looked at me and barked, 'Yauncey!' – that was his cook – 'Yauncey! She must must be hungry, go get some spam!' Spam! I hadn't heard the word since I was a child in North Carolina.

I looked around the house. It was definitely a mansion. Out behind the house was a huge pig-farm, the profits of which had paid for the building of the house, to C.C.'s design. My room was in one wing and C.C.'s in the other. There were chandeliers everywhere, each one holding dozens of candles. I lay in bed wondering what kind of place I had come to, and what would happen.

I was woken in the morning by the sound of men working below my bedroom window. They told me they were building a special extension to the house, a bedroom for the President to use when he came to officiate at C.C.'s and my wedding. I didn't know it, but C.C. was watching me while I talked to his men. He came to my bedroom before I was dressed and told me not to change out of the dressing gown I had on. I'd bought it in New York and I thought it was beautiful too – white silk patterned with lace right down to there. C.C. loved it: 'Wear it the whole time you're here,' he said, 'then my men will think we were in bed all night and I'll be able to control them better.'

I hadn't gone to C.C.'s room because I didn't know what the hell to do in order to make him hard. I got one of the drivers to take me to the nearest town so I could call Miriam and ask her advice, but I couldn't reach her in Kinshasa. I was going crazy about what I could do to encourage this wonderful old man. In the afternoon we went – with me still wearing my robe – to visit a woman newly widowed, the wife of a fellow mason friend of C.C.'s. I stayed outside and watched through the screen door as C.C. stood over her and made a long speech in praise of the dead man. The widow just sat looking down and as C.C. spoke her tears rolled down her face and dripped on to the floor, just like mine the previous night. She didn't make a sound. When he'd finished praising her husband C.C. gave her some money to help her get through. I cried too, but it was from relief – happy tears. I knew all the things I had suffered in America were over now. America itself seemed only a bad dream.

The next day C.C. gave me my reward for not drinking: Babycham, in little bottles with elephants on the label. By now my mood was so soft that I felt like someone could fold me up the size of a handkerchief and put me away in a drawer. When I wasn't crying with relief I worried over C.C. I had to sort out the sexual thing; if I couldn't settle that, there would be no marriage. It was the third day of my visit and I sat in the garden sipping Babycham and thinking. I got entirely lost in thought and when I looked up there were children all around me. One little boy had red hair, and I said, 'Don't you feel strange with your hair red?' He shook his head and replied, 'No, missy, I feel different, and I'm glad I'm different!' They asked me to teach them to read and write because they saw a letter I had from Lisa and they wanted to learn how to write like her. My heart went out to them.

That night I decided to go to C.C.'s bedroom. I had to, even though I wasn't sure what to do with this strange man. Everything was upside down and the wrong way round; out in the forest in this huge mansion I wasn't the same woman I was in my house by the ocean. It was a crazy atmosphere and I had no choice but to accept the strangeness and try to work out what to do with my prospective husband, who was the strangest of all.

C.C. never considered the possibility of me refusing him, and as the days slipped by it got to the point where I didn't know if I would ever be able to refuse him anything. But the big test, the first obstacle, was in his bed. I didn't have a clue what to do but there was no putting it off any longer, so I went to him.

It was not a success. I crept back to my own room sore, physically sore, and confused. I could marry this man, live in his crazy mansion and be happy doing it. As C.C.'s wife I could, if I wanted, be a respected member of Liberian society, part of the social circuit I knew from Monrovia. And when I got tired of that I could be the lady of the House in the Hills. The notion of spending the rest of my life that way, never playing in public again, never going back to America, stretched out before me and it was a serious notion, it was a real possibility. I knew C.C. meant what he said; if only I could bring him to life and make him feel man enough to want to take on a new wife.

That next morning I cried a lot. I didn't know what to do with him. So I sat at the kitchen table brushing my hair and cried. The next thing I knew I felt something on the back of the chair and when I turned round there was a little girl standing there. I said 'What's your name, darling?' She said 'Comfort,' and laid her hand on my shoulder. If I'd thought I'd been crying before, it was nothing to the tears that fell when this little angel told me her name. She stood by and watched as I wept myself dry, and when she saw I'd done she slipped away – I never saw her leave – and joined her friends outside.

Later that day as the evening approached, I began to get anxious. The idea of repeating the failure of the night before was too much and I jumped up from the dinner table, mumbling something about needing to get out of the house. 'Where you going, woman?' C.C. screamed – he always screamed when he talked. He said once that I could scream as much as I liked, he could always outscream me. It was pitch-black outside and I couldn't see a thing but I said, 'I'm going into town.' Off I went, tripping in the dark. C.C. sent Yauncey out

147

after me. He didn't try to stop me but walked a few yards behind the whole way into town, making sure I was all right. I hung around in the tiny town for a while and then walked back. 'Feel better now?' C.C. yelled when I returned. I did, I felt great.

The next morning was Sunday and I asked C.C. what he did on Sundays. He boomed, 'I dance! I've got a record player here. We will dance!' We danced all morning, and in the afternoon got ready to drive back to Monrovia. Just as we were about to leave a car drove up and four great fat women got out, all dressed in white, like the deaconesses at our church in Tryon back when I was a little girl. They looked at me and teased C.C., saying, 'Is this her, is this Nina?' He just grinned and they all took a good look at me, walking around to catch me from every angle. Then one of them said something to C.C. that I couldn't hear, and he roared with laughter, and so did the fat ladies. He came back to the car and I asked him what she'd said. 'You'd better fuck her good or she's gonna leave you,' C.C. replied.

We drove back, and I sat at home that night thinking about my crazy weekend. Life with C.C. was something I thought I could get used to but I needed help sorting him out, getting to be a proper wife in bed. So I went to see Martha Prout, my African momma. She seemed fascinated by what I had to tell her, and she went and got some wine and we talked long into the night. What I didn't know was that before I arrived in Liberia C.C. had been seeing Martha and there had been talk of her marrying him. And she still wanted him. So she filled me full of wine, I told her everything and she went straight off the next day and started to spread rumours about what I'd told her, using her knowledge against me.

I was completely ignorant of the plotting going on behind my back. Then I had what must be one of the stupidest ideas I ever had in my life; if Martha was no use in sorting out my problems with C.C., why not go home and ask my real momma? I was so concerned about C.C. the notion of going back to the USA didn't worry me. After all, I'd just see Momma and then come back with the knowledge which would get me C.C. So I left Lisa with C.C.'s daughter-in-law and flew to North Carolina.

I should have known America wouldn't let me get away so easily. I realized even before I saw Momma that it was an insane idea to ask her advice. I'd never talked about these sort of things with Momma in my entire life, and what did I expect her, a Methodist minister, to say? So I kept my mouth shut and just stayed with her a while. But as soon as people heard I was back they started calling me up. I stopped off in New York to see people, was invited upstate a couple of times and before I knew it four weeks had passed. I thought about C.C. the whole time but I had no answers so I put off my return, hoping inspiration would suddenly strike and I'd be able to go back with a definite plan.

I hadn't said anything about my trip to C.C., thinking I'd be back before he knew I was gone, but as my trip lengthened Martha Prout got to work, telling him I was gone for good, that I never cared for him, that I laughed at him behind his back, and, worst of all, that I'd left my daughter stranded in Liberia because I didn't care about her. With no one there to say otherwise, C.C. believed her. He wiped me from his mind. Martha, of course, was there to pick up the pieces and give him comfort.

I arrived back in Liberia almost a month after I'd left and C.C. was up country, uncontactable. Martha Prout was with him, and friends told me the stories they'd heard. I'd spoken about my problem to no one in Liberia except Martha, so everyone believed her lies because I wasn't around to put them right. C.C. didn't call even when he was back in town. The only thing I got was a message from him saying he never wanted to talk to me again. And I never did, except once, when I went to a big party after it had just been announced that C.C. and Martha Prout were to be married. C.C. and I came face-to-face. All he said was, 'How's your daughter?' I turned my back on him and walked away.

It's a funny thing, but my reaction to losing C.C. was similar to the way I felt after Daddy died: I never really believed it was over between us, especially during the time I stayed in Liberia. I lived there for two more years after he married Martha Prout, and it never struck me that C.C. and I were finished. I heard rumours from his estate that Martha walked about in an exact copy of the robe I had worn when I stayed there, a robe which C.C. had bought for her and insisted she wear the whole time. That story, and others like it, convinced me we had unfinished business which one day would be resolved. It was only after I left Liberia that the reality started to seep through. I only really started to miss C.C. three years after I last saw him, and it was only once he had died that I realized the height of my stupidity, the depth of my sorrow.

There was a military coup in Liberia in 1980 and Samuel Doe took power. President Tolbert was murdered in the presidential mansion and other people associated with the Government were rounded up and paraded naked through the streets of Monrovia. Then ten of them were taken down to the beach, tied to palm trees and shot. C.C.'s son was one of those ten men. Clarence, the man who first took me to The Maze, was another.

C.C. Dennis died two weeks later, his heart broken. Before he died he burnt his house to the ground so Samuel Doe's men couldn't take it. They say C.C. and Martha Prout were among those people paraded naked through the streets. It could have been me.

Malcolm; Martin; Daddy; C.C.; all the greatest men I have known have died, taken away before I was ready to leave them. I have a videotape of the execution of C.C.'s son, given to me by a Liberian official who escaped after Samuel Doe took over. I keep the tape in my apartment in Los Angeles, and when I'm feeling blue and thinking of C.C. I take it out and watch it again. The horror of it makes my memories of C.C. more real.

Chapter 10

I lost C.C. in 1974 but I stayed in Liberia for two more years. It was hard knowing he was around and hearing about him from mutual friends; the hardest part was staying friends with his daughter-in-law Doris Dennis, but I determined not to let him come between us. We walked on the beach one evening as I told her what had happened; we laughed, cried, and then everything was fine between us again.

I might not have had C.C. but I still had Lisa. Through the years I had tried – constantly – to be a mother to her, but our life together had been a series of partings and reunions, partings and reunions, with neither of us knowing how long it would be before we were separated once more. When she was very young Andy and I had taken Lisa on the road, but that stopped as soon as she reached school age. I was glad – touring was no life at all, never mind a normal family life. I wouldn't take a dog on the road through choice, much less my daughter.

So it had been hard for Lisa, sharing me with the music industry, the movement and her father. On tour I missed her endlessly, and when I got home I would go crazy trying to show her how much I loved her, trying somehow to work off my guilt. I would surround Lisa with a suffocating love in my effort to make her forget I'd ever been away. It was only when we left the USA that we had a chance to try and behave like an average mother and daughter. In Barbados and Liberia we were able to live normally and have fun without having to worry about the calendar on the wall.

Lisa was entirely happy in Liberia, at school and at home. Seeing her that way gave me comfort on those days when memories of C.C. crowded back in and I brooded on what I'd lost. In time I moved back into the Liberian high life. Miriam made sure I was kept busy whenever she was in Monrovia, and I started off on another set of adventures. At a party one night she introduced me to a Frenchman from the Central African Republic. We both felt the attraction right away. It was a passionate affair, as hot as I had ever known, and we did crazy things together.

One night he asked me if I wanted to go to the movies. I said yes and he turned up driving a borrowed car. I didn't know he could drive, had never seen him in a car before, but he said it was fine and I jumped in. The truth was he had never been at the wheel of a car before in his life. We flew down the dark roads with him laughing and me feeling a mixture of elation and terror. At last, inevitably, we crashed. We went off the road and tumbled over into a ravine; the car came to a stop upside down about thirty feet below. We both crawled out of the wreck without a scratch and caught a lift back into town. He was still laughing.

A couple of days later seventeen Liberian policemen appeared at my door. They had heard about the wreck and wanted to question me about it. As we talked I realized they were more concerned that my boyfriend was originally French than anything else. One of them said, 'What's the matter, Miss Simone, don't you like Liberian men?' I said sure I did, but they didn't look convinced. They went off to talk it over and then one came back and said, 'Miss Simone, the only way to solve this is to put him out of the country.' So they did. They took him into jail for a day and deported him the next morning. Our affair was over.

A few days later one of the policemen came round to my house, walked in, took off his shoes and sat down. I looked at him. 'You liked the Frenchman,' he said. 'You're gonna like me too, because I'm not going home.' I got scared and ran over to Doris Dennis's house. She came back with me, reprimanded the guy and threw him out. That was the last I had to do with the Liberian police. I knew how cops behaved in the USA – I'd married one after all – but Liberian law enforcement was a whole new experience.

When strange episodes like the seventeen policemen happened I didn't worry too much. It was a question of accepting that in Africa events have their own logic, and you'll only be able to relax once you realize that. I met plenty of foreigners so uptight about being in Africa that they never opened their eyes and saw it for what it was. Closed hearts and minds.

Although I wished we could stay in Liberia for ever I was getting concerned about Lisa's education. She was settled in a school in

Monrovia, a good school, but I wanted her to move to a better one out in the country. She wouldn't hear of it, and we started having big fights about it. The more we argued the more conscious I became of a telephone conversation I'd had with Prime Minister Earl Barrow when I was in New York. After a while he had started talking about Lisa and about how difficult it must be for her to see only her mother or father at any one time, and how strange she must feel moving around from place to place. He suggested I should put Lisa in a boarding school for three years; it would give her stability, and I would be able to plan my own future knowing that Lisa was taken care of. Deep down I knew he was right, and it seemed to me that if Lisa was going to get so upset about a local move I might as well get the unpleasant business over with and put her in a school where she could settle down properly.

My mind set, I found a school in Switzerland, enrolled Lisa for the next term and started to organize our move. Earl Barrow had advised me not to see her while she was at school, in fact to leave her alone for those three years so that she could learn to be independent; but the thought of not seeing my daughter for so long was more than I could bear. Much as I loved Liberia I knew I wouldn't be happy if I stayed in the knowledge that Lisa was thousands of miles away, alone, in a cold white country. So I moved to Switzerland with her.

Just as I was ready to leave Liberia I was introduced to an East African man who had arrived in Liberia via Chicago. His name was Imojah. He owned a farm in East Africa but had fallen out of favour with his government so had decided to leave his home country for a while until things sorted themselves out. He was also a writer, and spent his exile working on the book that his farm responsibilities had always stopped him from finishing. Imojah was about six feet six, thin, dark-skinned, with a voice like bells and large hands. I have never met anyone like him sexually, before or since. He didn't even have to touch me sometimes – just being near him was enough. Half an hour after we had met we were in bed, and it was the most natural and inevitable thing in the world.

Imojah was like a slap in the face from fate – coming to Liberia when he did, just after I had made all the arrangements to go to Switzerland and Lisa had finally been persuaded to go. All of a sudden the hundred days before we were due to leave started to fly past, and as the deadline grew closer and closer the thought of leaving Imojah mixed up with my feelings for Liberia and turned into one great ball of pain.

Everything I saw – the beach, the sun, the rain coming in from the sea, my friends – reminded me I was leaving it all behind, and it broke my heart. When we finally flew out of Monrovia to Geneva I cried more than Lisa. I thought I was crying for Imojah but I realize now I was crying for Africa, for C.C., Imojah, my deported Frenchman, my friends, everything. Crying for a different life.

Imojah had promised to come and stay with us in Switzerland and write his book. The thought of seeing him again was some consolation as I settled into my newly rented house and prepared Lisa's things for her new school. We were both deep in shock at the huge difference between Liberia and Switzerland. The two places couldn't have been more different. Switzerland is rich, safe and very respectful of you so long as you have money. I had many fans there who would recognize me on the street and wave or say hello, and unlike the situation in America, I felt no real tension being surrounded by so many white people. After Liberia, however, it took a while getting used to white faces, and it took even longer for me to stop reacting to events and people like I had in Africa. I had to keep reminding myself I was back in Europe, where people are repressed and undemonstrative, and, in Switzerland at least, boring. The price you pay for living in safe and secure surroundings is loneliness. I swear all ten million Swiss citizens go to bed at exactly nine o'clock each night, including weekends. Each day is like the one before, and it gets greyer and greyer. If you see anybody at all it's only the same people as you saw yesterday.

It's a country that can drive you half-crazy just waiting for something to happen. That's what it did to me. Once Lisa had gone off to start her first term I wandered about the house fixing things up, moving the furniture and so on, but what I was really doing was waiting for Imojah. I was convinced he'd come. He'd said he would, and it had been so good between us I was sure he'd do anything to be there with me. I missed him and Liberia so badly I started to hallucinate that he was coming down the road: I'd look out of the window and see him walking towards the house, but by the time I got to the front door he was nowhere to be seen. Sometimes I'd run down the road looking behind trees and cars, trying to find out where he was hiding because I was so sure I'd seen him. Other times I'd see him out of the corner of my eye and whip round, only to find him gone. These hallucinations came and went for two or three months, and by the end of them all I knew was Imojah was never going to come and I was so lonely I didn't think I could bear it.

Thanks to the doctor in Liberia I at least had Daddy to talk to when things got bad, and if his spirit hadn't been around to comfort me I might have died there – just shrivelled away. I had never lived in Europe before and I didn't feel relaxed or at home as I had in Liberia and Barbados. Whenever I'd been in Europe before I'd been touring with Andy and my musicians and stage crew – all the paraphernalia of life on the road. Now I was alone. I had no intention of performing in the near future, and most of my close friends were in Africa. I'd lost contact with a lot of my friends in America through my determination to cut myself off from everything to do with the country that had betrayed me.

After my years in Liberia it wasn't easy to pick up where I'd left off before, and I found a lot of people had moved on while I was away. Friends from the movement had spread out all over the world and had taken new directions, had started families or had got involved in academic programmes, all activities which changed them from the people I remembered. And away from Africa and without the support of a successful career I became less confident; I started to change back to the shy woman I had been in New York in the early sixties. Without the movement to push me on and without the constant demands for interviews, photographs and public appearances, my introversion, my insecurity, which I'd managed to keep hidden for so long, came to the surface once again.

Word got round that I had moved to Europe – in the music business, agents and promoters know what you're doing before you've even decided to do it – and I started getting offers to perform. All the problems with royalties, record labels and the companies that had been set up when I was with Andy were still around and once I was more easily contactable I started hearing from lawyers and accountants telling me one thing or another, threatening this, promising that, wanting me to give them information about things that had happened years ago that I had nothing to do with at the time. I started to understand something about how the music industry works; if they want to steal from you they throw up smokescreens of lawyers, accountants and executives to try and confuse you enough to get you to call it all off. Those guys change jobs every time the sun goes behind a cloud, and every time you think you're getting somewhere with someone he moves on and you're left trying to pick up the pieces with some other schmuck. My financial affairs were so tangled it would take a whole team of lawyers for ever to sort them out; the people who were spending the money I earned and releasing records in my name without my permission knew that, and were just waiting for me to say, 'To hell with it' and quit. And if that wasn't enough, the Internal Revenue Service were still sniffing at my door, asking me questions about money I had earned while Andy was my manager – money I had never seen.

It seemed as though everywhere I looked problems jumped out at me. I had to escape, so on an impulse I flew down to Liberia to see Imojah and find out if he was ever going to come to Europe. Being back in Africa was almost too much to bear, seeing my old friends again, going down to the beach to look at my house. But Lisa was sixteen and in school; I'd made the choice to leave and now I had to live with it. Imojah was something else I'd have to learn to do without. He was pleased to see me but wasn't going anywhere, especially Europe; Liberia had him under its spell. 'I can't leave,' he said. 'I'm too happy here and Switzerland is too cold.' I almost begged him, but his mind was set.

My flying visit extended day by day as I put off my return home – I was looking for an excuse to stay. One afternoon I went to a party and met a businessman called Winfred Gibson, a Liberian. We got to talking and laughing, having a good time. When the conversation came round to what I was doing I told him how difficult it was for me, starting up my career again without the right organization, without anyone to take care of business. On the spot Winfred proposed himself as my sponsor – not as my manager exactly but as someone who would look after that side of things, leaving me free to concentrate on performing and earning enough to get myself a proper home in Europe. He was due to leave for London shortly, and he invited me to accompany him, to the Carlton Tower Hotel, where he would put me up in a suite while he lined up a series of deals – a record deal, concert tours and so on.

Within a few days we arrived in London and I took up residence in the suite Winfred had promised. He talked of a good future and seemed to be working hard at getting things together. It's important to understand that he was never a boyfriend – this was strictly a business relationship. The days passed, and whilst I preferred living in London to Switzerland, I started to get impatient, wanting to see some results rather than just listen to his big talk. After ten days or so I was downstairs in the hotel when the manager asked me to step into his office. As politely as he could, he asked when I was intending to pay the bill for myself and Mr Gibson. I looked at him and said I thought Mr Gibson had taken care of it – he had certainly told me he had. The manager shook his head.

I tried to talk to Winfred about the bill for most of that day but he was always busy – always working on some deal or slipping out for a meeting. Finally he came to my room and I asked what was going on. I reminded him he had invited me to London at his expense – otherwise why would I be living in a hotel when I was renting a house in Switzerland? And could he please tell me why he hadn't paid any of the hotel bills – not just mine, what about his own? By this time we were yelling at each other. After I asked him this final question he moved across the room and struck me. He rabbit-punched me on the neck and I was unconscious before I hit the floor.

When I woke up a while later, the room was empty. I could hardly move, I couldn't stand up, and I had to crawl over to the telephone like a dog and pull the receiver off the table on to the floor before I could use it. I called down to the front desk for help. Eventually the hotel nurse arrived. I couldn't tell her what had happened – I was so shocked – but she saw what pain I was in and, after helping me on to the bed, gave me an injection to knock me out. I woke up again hours later to find my room had been ransacked and all my money had gone. I never knew who did it.

I got on the phone again and insisted the hotel call the police. I wanted Winfred Gibson punished for what he'd done to me, and I wanted them to find whoever had stolen my money. The hotel didn't want the police to come, but I insisted. I couldn't move off the bed and the policemen interviewed me as I lay there, drugged and confused. I watched their faces as I talked, and realized they didn't believe a word I was saying. All they saw was this crazy woman with her eyes bigger than saucers lying with her neck at a strange angle and talking about a man they'd never heard of, whom the hotel said couldn't be traced right at that minute. They wouldn't arrest anyone, they said, not just on my say-so. Didn't I know this was England and they didn't do things like that?

I knew what they meant: they weren't going to get involved in a dispute between foreigners, especially black foreigners. And they weren't going to take the word of a woman against a man. They left.

I could hardly speak, I was in such pain and so upset. I sent the hotel staff away and lay on the bed crying. I was so alone – there wasn't a single person in the whole country I could call for help. I had no money, I could hardly move, and if I tried to leave the hotel I would be arrested for not paying the bill. My career as a musician was slowly falling to pieces because I had no organization, and I couldn't stay in my own country for more than a couple of weeks before I had to flee like a runaway slave. The men that might have saved me had died or were lost.

I thought of Imojah, who had seemed something definite to hold on to amidst the chaos of the rest of my life. Even he was gone, and now I didn't have the hallucinations to console me. I felt like I'd come to nothing, just another lonely woman stuck in a hotel bedroom in an unfriendly land. I reached over to the table at the side of the bed and took hold of my bottle of sleeping pills. I counted out thirty-five and took them, one by one.

I woke up in hospital with a sore stomach, my neck in a brace and all the papers full of news of my suicide attempt. One of the hotel staff had come back into my room to ask some questions about insurance, found me and called an ambulance. It was now thirty-six hours later. I lay there thinking. I was glad I hadn't died; at least, I thought, I couldn't get any lower than this – it would be uphill from now on.

I spent a couple of weeks recovering on a health farm a little way outside London and as I sat in my room – with a plaster brace around my neck – I thought carefully about what I was, and what I could do to get some control over my life. If I went home I'd be stuck between a rock and a hard place, going out of my mind in Switzerland wishing I'd stayed in Liberia, missing Imojah, knowing at the same time that if I gave in to the slimy charms of promoters begging me to perform – they always said it was because my public was so anxious to see me again, not because they wanted to make a lot of easy money – then I'd be going back into the dirty, dishonest world I'd left America to escape. I also knew Switzerland was no friend to the poor; I had at least some money – less as each day went by – which was why I was made so welcome: there was no other reason. But I wasn't getting what was mine by right from the States, and Switzerland wasn't

Liberia – I wasn't being given places to live for free, I wasn't a guest of honour. In the end, I decided to give into the pressure and start performing in public again, to preserve my sanity and keep myself solvent.

I played a few shows in France, Holland, Germany and even Switzerland. I had no manager and no proper lawyer in Europe, nor a regular agent. Most of the work I did myself, with the occasional help of enthusiastic fans who wanted to be my saviour in a couple of weeks and always ended up sending my suitcases to Italy when I was flying to Spain, forgetting my make-up – annoying stuff like that. I did sometimes work with professional agents, but we always fell out after a few weeks either because they were crooks or because we just didn't hit it off personally. Nobody seemed to think it possible I didn't feel like I was born to perform, that I might not like performing unless everything about it was done properly. I had been an artist too long to find dirty dressing rooms romantic, screw-ups funny and thieving low-life promoters 'colourful characters'. I hated every minute of most of those shows.

Only the good audiences made it worthwhile, on those nights when they showed respect and love and between us we pushed through to something higher. All I knew about performing was confirmed by those European concerts; without the right staff and right off stage routines nothing would happen on stage, and whether or not you had the right staff, the only thing you should trust is your own instinct.

Some nights my audiences weren't fans but curiosity-seekers who had come to see if I was as difficult as the press said I was – difficult because I objected when people weren't punctual, or didn't take any notice of my instructions for the staging, or didn't tune my piano properly, or didn't pay me the agreed sum at the contracted time. An audience uninterested in what you have to offer as an artist is the easiest thing in the world to recognize; you feel it the moment you walk out on to the stage.

I played at the MIDEM festival in Cannes, in front of that kind of audience. MIDEM is a sort of music industry convention, so the crowd that night weren't just everyday people – they were mostly from the music industry, and they came to see me fail because they knew what I thought of their business and they hated me for speaking out in public about it. It was quite a show. They booed during songs and shouted out in the silences; they wouldn't let me compose myself between songs; and when they saw that they couldn't intimidate me that way they just sat quietly, refusing to applaud. A few real fans had somehow managed to get through the security on the door and they helped me out as much as they could, but it was no use. In the end I just stood up, said what I thought of them and their business and walked off. The silence was deafening.

There was a great fuss about this show throughout Europe because all the music press were in town for the convention. Some papers – like the *Melody Maker* in England – understood what I was saying and were sympathetic, but most condemned me. The press and the music industry found it difficult to accept that I didn't give a damn about those people and what they represented. They expected me to be grateful just to be on stage in front of them, they thought I should feel honoured. I didn't. The only thing I felt when I walked off stage was that I needed to take a bath as soon as possible, to wash their dirt off my skin. This was what I'd left Africa for?

In the middle of all the controversy I got a call from Andy. He wanted me to do a small US tour with him as my manager, strictly professional, no strings, just to see how it would go. My feelings towards him were deep and complicated, but whatever else I thought of him I knew he was the best organizational manager I had ever had, and he knew I knew that.

On the road with Andy things ran like clockwork, and I'd never questioned that side of his work. The idea of the tour was attractive; it would be easier than working on my own in Europe, the money was good and I'd get to see friends in New York again. And maybe – maybe – Andy and I would find a way of working together on a purely professional level. If we did, that would solve a lot of my problems. I had no illusions, but I was willing to give it a try. Al Schackman was keen on the idea, too, and he and my other favourite musicians would be on the tour with me. So I agreed, and flew to New York.

I cleared customs at the airport and walked through into the arrivals lounge. The press were waiting for me there – reporters, photographers, the whole thing – plus a few dozen fans who'd heard I was coming and came to greet me with flowers and other small gifts. I hadn't played in New York for a while and the tour was due to finish at Carnegie Hall and the Newport Jazz Festival. So there was a lot of interest in my arrival, as well as people wanting to know where I'd been for so long and what I'd been doing in Africa. The fans had copies of the *New York Times*, which was carrying the news of my arrival.

I stopped to answer questions from the press, and I was astonished when they started saying things like, 'Nina, do you think you'll have to go to jail?' I looked at Andy, who was obviously feeling a little uncomfortable. 'How'll you plead, Nina?' another guy asked. I looked at the paper. The story wasn't just about my first concert in New York for a while; it went on to say how I was to appear in court as soon as I arrived, accused of failing to file my yearly tax returns, and with the possibility of other more serious charges to follow. I knew nothing at all about this. What had seemed like a welcome return to my country had turned into a squalid press scandal. Andy, all smiles, reassured me that everything would be all right. He said we'd have to go to court for three days before the tour started, but he had a good lawyer and I'd get off.

The years in question included my last years under Andy's management, but I noticed I was the only one who was going before a judge in open court, for the whole city to read about. I felt ashamed.

Before I went to court we had a meeting with the district attorney, and he offered me a deal. If I pleaded guilty to not filing tax returns for the first two years then they'd drop charges for the second two.

Under advice, I agreed. Just being in the Justice Building frightened me. That night I woke up screaming, not knowing where I was. I should have known: Brooklyn, New York, USA – the place I had run away from.

The next day it was my turn in the District Court. I was lucky to have Judge Constance Baker Martland presiding, one of the most distinguished black female justices in America. She saw how scared I was and tried to be as compassionate as she could. The lawyers went through their stuff, and judgement was postponed to a later date pending more legal technicalities.

I was supposed to be free to go, but they took me down underneath the courts to some kind of holding facility. There was a man down there dressed in black and white, an ugly, very white man, white as if he didn't ever go out in the daytime. I'll never forget his face. He grabbed hold of me and said, 'You're in jail now. Gimme that pocketbook you got – I think you've got a gun in there!' Then he fingerprinted me.

He wasn't supposed to do it, but he did and laughed while he did it. He had a real southern drawl in his voice and he mispronounced my name on purpose, calling me 'Nine-ah.' He said, 'You're name is Nine-ah, isn't it? Nine-ah, and you're from the south. Well, I am, too, and you'd better understand that you're in jail now, you're not in court. You're in jail until we let you out.' I was terrified. My lawyer was gone and I'd been left alone. I screamed for Andy but he was gone too, nowhere to be seen. Eventually the guy let me out, just as my lawyer came down to find out what was going on. Andy came in a moment later, saying he'd been in the men's room all that time. I didn't believe him. I think when the guy started to take my fingerprints he thought they were going to arrest me on further charges and take me away, and he didn't want to be there if they did – he didn't want me to see his face. When we first went into that room he was right there with me but he vanished as soon as the trouble started. I just looked around and he was gone.

I knew right then the tour was a mistake. It seemed to me that Andy had changed over the years; he was less willing to exercise the control that he used to have over every aspect of touring, every little thing. My first clue to this was when he sent a man I didn't know to pay me – he wouldn't sit down and sort out the money with me himself. That was never how we had done things. I might have been a little naive to expect things to be exactly as they were, but, naive or not, it was a shock to me, and I was thrown off balance.

Things didn't run smoothly at all; there were no major disasters, but it wasn't much better than my own dates in Europe. The difference was the pressure I was under, not just from the tax charges – which still had to be cleared up – but from the general unease I felt about playing in America once again. After Switzerland and Cannes my nerves were very delicate, and the whole reason for accepting the tour was to be able to work under the protection of a proper manager again, to have a chance to get myself together. As the Carnegie Hall date approached I realized I had made a big mistake in coming to America at all. Judge Constance Baker Martland found me guilty as charged and imposed a fine, which Andy said he would take care of. He didn't, and my tax problems in the USA would take another ten years to sort out.

My nervousness increased; the court judgement was partly responsible for that, but most of all it was being in America again, with Andy, stirring up all the old memories I wasn't ready to face. At last I couldn't stand it any longer and caught a cab to the airport. I was desperate to get out, to get back home, wherever that was. Carnegie Hall and the Newport Jazz Festival would have to wait a little longer before they saw me again. My greatest regret was letting down George Wein – the promoter – who had been a faithful supporter of mine over the years.

When I fled from New York he had to cancel the shows at very short notice and refund all the ticket money – the shows had sold out – and I would have understood if he'd been furious. He wasn't, he was very kind, and he issued a press release saying he regretted my actions but understood the pressure I was under. It was a very generous thing for George to say, and I've never forgotten it.

I arrived back in Europe knowing I couldn't go back to America until I felt totally prepared, and that if I lived much longer in Switzerland I would go insane. I played a few jazz festivals in the summer but I was just drifting, trying to find something to hold on to amidst all the uncertainty. I had started up my musical career almost by accident, simply because I happened to be living in countries where people wanted to see me perform, and it was totally the wrong way to go about doing things – agreeing to perform first and thinking about getting the right staff together second. I hadn't really got out of my African frame of mind and I'm sure the Swiss and everyone else thought I was crazy. My mind was full of memories of Imojah, C.C. and Daddy. C.C. especially, as I realized the security I had thrown away by losing him.

I played the Festival Hall in London and immediately afterwards was asked to tour Israel. I felt it was exactly what I needed – to go to the Holy Land, get in touch with myself and with God, and think things through. Best of all, the tour was arranged so I could be in Bethlehem on Christmas Day. I called Momma to tell her, and for once she was pleased to hear my plans. I flew to Tel Aviv with Max Cohen – my lawyer for all those years – and his wife. I fell asleep on the El Al plane after we took off and when I woke up there was a line of people standing in the aisle, queueing up. I thought they were waiting to use the bathroom or something, but they were all standing looking at me, waiting for me to wake up so they could hug and kiss me and welcome me to their country. They said they had been waiting for me to come for over ten years. The newspapers were full of the news of my arrival, and when I got off the plane the Mayor of Tel Aviv was

163

waiting to greet me. The crowds were incredible, both fans and press. It took us four hours to get away from the airport, straight to a civic reception.

The whole thing gave me the kick I needed, and after playing the first show I just relaxed and drove around the Holy Land, taking in the spiritual atmosphere. I visited all the biblical places and stood in the church in Bethlehem on Christmas Day with all the other worshippers – people from every country you can imagine. I played another concert in Tel Aviv in the New Year, and I was so relaxed I drifted away on the music – drifted right out of consciousness for a while. The audience came down out of their seats on to the stage and swayed around to the music. When I woke up out of my dream state I saw them crying and they came up and kissed me, begging me to stay. I asked them what had happened while I was high on the music, but they wouldn't tell me.

For the first time in what seemed like forever I enjoyed both performing and travelling in a new country, and I left Israel refreshed. I felt as if my luck was about to change: mostly that was because I'd realized something very important while I was in the Holy Land; I had nobody to rely on but myself and my father's spirit, and I was going to have to get used to the fact. In time I grew to almost like the idea – Daddy would be my only companion until a man his equal came along, and we both knew that meant I might have to wait a long, long time.

Chapter 11

Telling yourself things are going to get better is one thing but making them so is something else. I left Israel at the start of 1979 determined to turn things around but without too much idea of exactly what I could do. If I was going to perform regularly – and I needed to, in order to earn money – then I had to have the right people around me. I couldn't rely on old friends, ex-husbands or smooth-talking business-men – 1978 had taught me that.

I decided the first thing I had to do was move away from Switzerland; the place depressed me so much. I realized I needed to live in a busy city, a place where I could go out and enjoy myself rather than stay at home staring at the walls and thinking about lost loves, lost chances.

As I wasn't going to be playing in America in the near future, if I was going to pick up my career again it would have to be in Europe. So I packed up the few things I had – most of my possessions were still in Liberia, Barbados or the USA – and moved to Paris.

I'd started to learn French when I was in Switzerland and had been performing in French for many years – the day I discovered the songs of Jacques Brel was one of the most exciting in my whole life – so Paris seemed to make sense. The French also have a lot of respect for serious artists: they are not too bound up in the commercial side of the music industry and you are still admired and popular even if you don't happen to have a record in the pop charts at any particular moment. Paris also has a wonderful African community, containing people from every country on the continent, so I would be able to create my own Africa in the heart of Europe, Africa in my mind.

I arrived alone and rented a small apartment. When I started to look around for concert work all sorts of promoters immediately made offers, but always on the condition that I signed up with them, let them handle the money, did what they said. I was determined to make it work on my own so I turned them all down. At last I managed to get myself a booking, at a tiny club in the Pigalle called Les Trois Maillets. I knew it wasn't much of a place, but I figured that once people knew I was there they'd come to see me play, the place would sell out and I'd get offered something better. I remember what I said to myself as I waited in my dressing room – if you could call the tiny cupboard I had a dressing room – on my first night. 'Don't worry, Nina,' I said. 'It's not for long.'

Les Trois Maillets was not much bigger inside than the old Midtown Bar in Atlantic City. It had a little raised stage at the back of a long room and no proper ventilation, so the cigarette smoke hung out across the stage, getting thicker and thicker as the night went on. I could actually feel my throat drying as I played and I knew that before too long the smoke would start to affect my voice. Looking out into the crowd I heard Jimmy Baldwin's voice in my head, 'This is the world you have made for yourself, Nina, now you have to live in it.'

The fans I expected, the crowds which would lift me out of a seedy club in the Pigalle and into the Olympia Theatre and beyond, never materialized. I couldn't understand it; all my life, no matter what problems I might have been having in my personal life I always pulled an audience, I always sold out.

It was only later that I understood. The French admired me not only as a musician but as a star, in the same way that they loved Edith Piaf, and they didn't separate the life from the music. Most audiences expect a performer to go on stage, to play the songs they like and maybe a couple of new ones; then they go home content, thinking their ticket money well spent. The French, especially Parisians, aren't like that at all; they demand that a star lives the life of a star every minute of the day. So they expected me to be staying in a luxury suite at the Georges Cinq Hotel and to be seen at celebrity parties, and they wanted to read about me in the society pages. If I didn't do that, then in their eyes I wasn't the same person – I wasn't Nina Simone the star, the person they would queue for hours to see. Many of my French fans – and I know this because they told me – simply didn't believe it was me playing in that little club on the Pigalle. Or if they did believe it they thought I was going through some private troubles and, in a sense, didn't like to intrude on my grief – they wouldn't come to see me when I was down. I sort of love and hate the French for that; they didn't come because they respected me, but because they didn't come I couldn't rise up from the place I had fallen to. Later, when I did go back to the Georges Cinq and I did play the Olympia Theatre, they lined up around the block to buy tickets and gave me a ten-minute ovation the moment I walked on stage. *C'est la vie.*

'This is the world you have made yourself, now you have to live in it.' Jimmy's words became the motto of my life over the next couple of years. I was determined not to give in. I wasn't earning enough to live on at the club, and my savings – what little I had – gradually trickled away. I came to regard these days in Paris as my fall from grace, a sort of punishment, but for what I didn't know. I had to sell my car, my furniture and my jewels. Lisa meanwhile left school and flew back to the USA to be with her father; I thought she'd come back to Europe, but she didn't – she said she'd decided to go to college in America.

Bad times, but I wasn't unhappy. I had virtually nothing, but I knew what little I had and I learned to accept things the way they were. I didn't lie awake at night thinking about the money that had been stolen from me, or the people who had lied to me. And as time passed I learned not to think too often of C.C. or Imojah. What kept me sane was knowing that things would change, and it was a question of keeping myself together until they did.

I wasn't the only person suffering; news started to emerge about the coup in Liberia – this was in 1980 – and I heard terrible stories, not only about C.C. and his son, but about many of my friends, and their children. I imagined the bodies of the executed officials lying in the sand on the beach outside my house, tied to the palm trees I used to sit under drinking palm wine, laughing. Paris was bad, but there were worse places to be.

Whilst I was first living in Paris I had recorded an album on Creed Taylor's CTI record label, *Baltimore.* Creed Taylor offered me the record and, although I didn't particularly enjoy recording it, I knew it would help push my career along.

I had this in mind when I played a concert in the south of France in the summer of 1981. Part of the deal I made was that the promoter gave me the right to sell the videotape he made of the concert. I picked up the tape and flew to LA to see if I could sell it to one of the record companies out there. At first LA seemed as difficult as Paris – closed doors and unhelpful telephone conversations – and I started to wonder at the point of it all. Then I called a smaller video company, Videopix, and everything changed.

I talked to the president of the company, a man named Anthony Sannucci, and he invited me downtown to talk about distributing my tape. We sat in his office drinking coffee and talking not just about the tape but about what I'd been doing over the past few years, what I wanted to do in the future, and how I might go about it. I explained that I had no management because I wanted to do things on my own, to be responsible to no one.

'I understand what you're saying,' he said. 'But, Nina, I don't think you can do it – not with the music business being the way it is right now.'

I disagreed, and he held up his hands. 'Okay, if that's what you want, that's fine. But if ever you are looking for a manager, you know where we are.' I flew back to Paris feeling good; at least I'd had some success – even though Anthony Sannucci hadn't committed to releasing the tape, it was nice to know that somebody believed in me and wanted to get involved. I could see Sannucci – as I called him from our first meeting on – was interested in money first, last and in between. If he wanted to manage me it was because he knew he could make money doing it.

On the plane back to Europe I thought about his offer again, turning it over in my mind. I was due to start recording another album in Paris – which was eventually released as *Fodder in Her Wings* – and I realized with a start that it was nearly three years since I'd recorded the album *Baltimore*, and I'd been living in Paris even longer than that. Four years – of waiting for the wheel to come around and lift me up once more – had passed.

Lisa, to my surprise, had in the end decided not to go to college and had joined the US Army instead. She wrote occasionally, but our relationship was complicated and difficult. Too much had happened between us and I had never spent the time I should have done with her when she was younger. There was no way I could make her understand how I just never had the time and how much I wished that I had. 'This is the world you have made . . .'

I began to wonder if I had done the right thing in turning down Sannucci. Over the following weeks I looked hard at the life I had, and remembered how when Andy was managing me I never had to call promoters or hassle record companies to chase royalties, and never had to book my own hotels or flights. I knew my performances suffered now, because I used up all my energy off stage just getting to the concert hall. There were dozens of good reasons to hand over my management to someone else, but still I hesitated. In the end it took me most of 1982 to make up my mind.

In between times I played a couple of concert dates in London but pulled out of the rest of the British shows I had booked. I sat in my hotel room and realized I couldn't carry on with the tour – my nerves wouldn't allow it. Every now and then I felt a strangeness tugging at the edges of me, and I remembered what had happened to me on the Cosby tour back in the sixties, when I started having visions through overwork. Now I was doing the same sort of tours without any of the staff that I'd had then, and at times it was very hard keeping myself together.

I was like a child hesitating on the edge of a swimming pool, not quite daring to jump in. In the end something that had nothing to do with my life as a performer pushed me over the brink: Earl Barrow died in Barbados. He had been out of office for nearly ten years – outvoted while I was in Liberia – and had campaigned tirelessly for re-election.

His doctors had advised him to slow down, but asking Earl to give up politics was like asking a fish to give up water. He fought his last great election and won, becoming Prime Minister again, but died almost immediately, of a massive heart attack. When Al Schackman heard about it, he turned to me and said, 'The once and future king', and that's what Earl Barrow was – in or out of office he was a king among men.

I hadn't seen Earl for years – I went back to Barbados once but he was in the middle of an election and couldn't see me. But when he died I suddenly felt more alone than I could remember, and it made me more aware than ever that time was passing, and with it opportunities. I called Sannucci and he flew over to Paris to fetch me. Back in LA I rented an apartment from him and we started work on a new album and began planning new tours to Europe and around the States, which Sannucci somehow managed to square with the IRS. Sannucci had an associate, a man named Eddie Singleton, who was a musician and record producer. Things were arranged so that Sannucci took care of the money and Eddie oversaw the album project.

If Paris had been my fall from grace, then Sannucci was my

penance; I liked the man, liked him very much, but you had to understand how he worked. Sannucci liked money; he was a wealthy man – one of the richest I know – and he got that way by being as ruthless as necessary when he had to be. It wasn't that he was greedy, not at all, it was more that the idea of turning his back on a good deal was incomprehensible to him.

I never played poker with Sannucci, but I guarantee that he would play as hard for one dollar as he would for a million. At the same time he was generous with his own money. Some weeks he'd get bored, call me up and say 'Nina, let's go to Vegas!' We'd jump in his Mercedes and go play the tables, stop off at the track to bet on the horses and end up in a fine restaurant, toasting the day.

He regarded managing me as a kind of two-way bet; if he couldn't win commercially he was going to have fun trying. I had to watch him very carefully and check everything he told me. If I didn't, I could be certain he'd try to catch me out. Often, when I accused him of not being entirely straightforward he'd admit it with a smile and say, 'You're right! I thought you'd notice that!' For all Sannucci's tricks, he knew I was enjoying being part of an organization again, and having the responsibility for many of my concert and recording arrangements taken off my hands.

But the reason I most liked Sannucci was that he was lucky; he nearly always won whatever he gambled on, and he certainly struck lucky with me. A short while after we signed a management contract I started to hear news from Europe that 'My Baby Just Cares for Me', one of the tracks I'd recorded during the Bethlehem session in 1958, was becoming a hit everywhere.

Bethlehem had licensed the *Little Girl Blue* album to a European distributor and that particular song – one of the slightest I'd ever recorded – was released as a single and hit, first in the clubs and later in the charts. The song was also being used by an advertiser to help sell perfume right across continental Europe. All those years ago I'd signed the contract Sid Nathan stuck in front of me and given up my claim on almost everything my Bethlehem recordings had earned over the years. I was just a girl back then and knew nothing: it's probably cost me more money than I could count. But with the song hitting all over I knew this was the sign that my fall and penance were over. I knew too that this was a last chance; the opportunity to put my career back into high gear was staring me in the face, and I had to grab it.

Sannucci understood this too and we worked as hard as we could, playing concerts across Europe, appearing on TV shows, giving interviews. The greatest thrill was seeing young people in my audiences, kids like there had been in the Village, not caring what sort of music it was but just enjoying it. The more shows I played, the higher up the ladder I climbed, the more confident I became. And I had done it without pandering to the music industry. I still said the same things I always did, that the music industry is full of thieves, that America is a racist country and those black citizens who involved themselves in the movement were still being punished twenty years later.

After three stormy years I split from Sannucci. It wasn't an easy decision, but I'd changed through the time we were working together and he didn't understand that. He thought he knew everything about business and how an artist should behave, but compared to me he was a newcomer; I'd had twenty-five years experience of taking the heat off stage and on. As my records started to hit in Europe and I realized that my fans would always come out to see me, would always support me, I felt some of the self-confidence I'd lost during those slow months in Paris returning. I began to want to contribute more to the management side of my life, and that was where the problems started.

My new, more positive attitude was difficult for Sannucci to take because up to then I'd been happy to let him deal with everything. The first few times I opened my mouth he'd say, 'It's okay, Nina, this is business, let me take care of it.' He didn't want the competition that he saw me as, and he certainly didn't want to be put in the position where he might have to admit there were some things I knew more about than him. I wanted our relationship to be a partnership but he wasn't ready for that, and things started to heat up between us – slowly at first because I still liked the man, and wanted to work with him – until finally it all boiled over.

I had played at Ronnie Scott's club in London many times over the years, and the place was always packed tight. Ronnie's is a typical jazz club, which means the atmosphere is always great, the audiences crazy about me – sometimes too much, they would get so intense – but at the same time it can get very hot and smoky, and playing two sets, the jazz club way, was very hard work. I had to be very careful with my voice, so through the daytime I would hardly speak and I drank as much hot lemon and herb tea as I could to lubricate my throat. My second set would finish around 1.30 in the morning; I still had the same old problem coming down after a performance so I wasn't able to get any sleep until breakfast time some 6 or 7 hours later. It was like working a hard night shift on a factory floor and any performer, not just me, can only do that for so long before they need a rest.

We arrived in London this one time to play a week at Ronnie's. The demand for tickets was so great that Ronnie invited us to stay on for another week. I wasn't keen, but Sannucci persuaded me and the second week was announced. That week sold out, too, so Ronnie asked us if we'd like to extend to a third. Without telling me, Sannucci agreed. I was furious; not with Ronnie Scott's, who had simply asked a reasonable question, but with Sannucci. What he did was a snapshot of how he saw our whole relationship, that negotiating with a club was his job and any decisions made were on his say-so. Never mind that I was tired out and my voice was suffering, never mind that I was the one who actually had to go out and do the work. What made me even more mad was his assumption that he could take the decision and then get me to agree to it, no matter what.

Sannucci's mistake was that he didn't realize I was a different person from the woman who he had met in his office in LA a few years before. Back then I was so pleased to have people around to share my burden that I probably would have done the third week out of fear of annoying him so much he'd walk out on me. But those days had passed; not only was I more confident and secure but I was in the record charts throughout Europe and promoters there, in the USA and Canada, where I'd recently stayed for a few months, were calling up offering concerts, as well as countries like Japan and Australia. It was good to play at Ronnie Scott's and good to earn money there but it wasn't as if it was the only place in the world where I could do that, and it wasn't as if I needed to agree to play every engagement I was offered. Sannucci could have thanked Ronnie for this offer, said he was sorry to have to turn it down right then but would be happy to arrange a return booking sometime later in the year.

As it was, my throat was sore, I wasn't sleeping well and I needed a rest. I knew it wouldn't be fair on the fans who came to see me that week because I wasn't in top shape, and they'd be paying to watch a sub-standard performance.

But Sannucci wouldn't see it from my point of view. The bigger question was: who really made the important decisions about what happened in my life? We both knew this was what it was all about, and neither of us would give an inch. I said I wasn't going to play the extra week, and he said if I didn't then it was all over between us. It was like a game of chicken, each of us daring the other to give in. I think he didn't believe I was really serious, but he'd picked the wrong woman to bet against.

The first night of the third week I didn't show up and made sure he couldn't find me. Ronnie Scott's cancelled the rest of the week – they had no choice; I was sorry that they had been put in such a position but there was nothing else I could do and, good as his word, Sannucci flew back to LA without me. The whole thing was a terrible shame. I liked Sannucci and Ronnie Scott's had always been very good to me, but I knew I could manage on my own again, and that I had an audience which would not let me go – they had made 'My Baby' a hit without me even being on the same continent. So, my penance over, I left Sannucci – although we remained, and remain, friends – and started working with Raymond Gonzalez, whom I had known for a long time. At first Raymond was my agent in Europe, but over the years we found we could bear each other's company, so Raymond became my agent everywhere, which he remains to this day.

We've had good times together and over the years have played some wonderful concerts – for President Mitterand in a château in the Loire valley, at a gala evening in Paris where I wore a quarter of a million dollars' worth of Boucheron diamonds, and most memorably at an open-air bullring, a *plaza del toros*, in Spain, where the promoter wanted to cancel the show because it had rained all day and he was convinced no one would come out for the evening. Hardly any tickets had been sold in advance and this poor guy was sure he was going to lose his shirt. 'Don't worry, people will come,' I said. By the time I went on stage there were 8,000 people there, crowding over the seats, hanging out of the balconies to cheer me as I walked out into the centre of the ring. The rain had stopped just long enough for everything to dry out and it was one of those lovely still evenings you get after the rain. As the sun went down everyone started to light the candles they had brought with them and I performed in the middle of a flickering universe, half out of my mind at the beauty of it all, with the promoter standing back in the shadows with tears in his eyes – probably in relief that his money was safe. But I knew, and after being on the road with me for a while Raymond did, too, that the people would come.

Raymond and I established a regular series of concerts throughout Europe and my mind turned away from the road back to my domestic life. I had an apartment in Hollywood, but that wasn't too much use when I had a week to burn in between dates in Europe. For the time being I'd had enough of Paris and what I needed was a quiet place to come home to where I could relax, and which would contrast with the hectic high-powered atmosphere of luxury hotels in capital cities.

Once, in the mid-sixties, I gave a concert in Central Park, New York. The movement was at its height at that time and both my performance and the audience that day was fiercely political. The crowds pressed close to the front of the stage and Andy, standing behind me in the wings, got worried that the stage would be crushed under the audience's collective weight and me along with it. He started to move me off the stage, helped by a young Dutch photographer, Gerrit De Bruin. From the audience's point of view it looked like my performance was being stopped by some unknown white man. They didn't understand what was really going on and pressed forward angrily. The stage started to buckle and we just made it to the Mercedes before the crowds surged in around us. Andy pushed Gerrit on to the floor of the car so they couldn't see him and we slowly pushed our way through the masses, holding our breath and hoping he wouldn't be noticed.

It was a terrifying experience and Gerrit and I became firm friends from that moment on. As time passed I came to rely on him more and more. Soon after Andy and I had split up, I was stuck in Europe feeling down. Gerrit saw my mood, packed me and my suitcases into his little car, and we set off on a driving tour, staying in small hotels without calling up to make reservations, eating in tiny restaurants in alpine villages. Every so often people would think they recognized me but then dismiss the notion because they thought there was no way Nina Simone would be seen in the sort of places we were in. Gerrit and I had a wonderful time, and coming when it did it saved my skin. As I started to look around for a home base in Europe Gerrit suggested I buy an apartment in Nijmegen, Holland, close to where he lived. I liked the idea and Gerrit helped me to move in and took care of all the hundreds of problems that turn up when you move to a new country. He came on the road with me as well, sorting out problems in his same calm and unflustered way. Gerrit was and is the proof of something I've always known: that I've been lucky in my friends.

Once my career stabilised I had time to sort out some of the more worrying problems that had stayed with me from the sixties. After years of legal arguments I finally made peace with IRS, which meant I could live, travel and perform in the USA again without worrying I'd have to face another trial. I journeyed back to both Barbados and Liberia – where I was welcomed just as warmly as I had ever been – and laid to rest the various ghosts which had haunted me. C.C., Imojah, Earl Barrow – all became memories, sad memories, but memories, not ghosts who flitted through my days distracting me from the business of living in the present. Once America opened to me again I started to re-establish contact with friends from the movement: on 21 January 1991 I marched in the parade to celebrate Martin Luther King's birthday, alongside friends from those years: Andy Young, John Lewis, Coretta Scott-King and many, many others. Like me, they had all gone through changes – not all of them for the good – but walking together that day we celebrated not just Martin's birthday but ourselves, that we had all made it through.

Daddy, too, slowly slipped away. His spirit had been around me when I needed him most but as my career improved, as I became wealthier and started to buy properties in Hollywood and Europe, as I took the opportunity to take the holidays I'd always promised myself – luxury cruises, safaris – Daddy's spirit moved into the background, leaving me to enjoy new friends.

Spending so much time in Europe I got a little tired of the quiet life in Nijmegen so I moved to Amsterdam, to a penthouse apartment next to a canal. I threw a party to announce my arrival in town and my social life became hectic immediately, a rush of dinners, cocktail parties and theatre openings.

But what I like most of all about the way things are now is that I have enough financial security to know that I can't be pushed into doing anything I don't want to. When I release a new album or video it'll be because I'm proud and want to share it – no other reason.

Momma is just the same as she ever was, devout and feisty, the one constant, for better or worse, in my whole life. Miz Mazzy died just a few years ago, aged 102, and everyone in Tryon paid their respects at her funeral.

Right now I'm as close to happy as I can be without a husband to love, I started to work on this book, looking back over a life which, after thinking about for months and months, I have no regrets about. Plenty of mistakes, some bad days, and, most resonant of all, years of joy – hard, but joyous all the same – fighting for the rights of my brothers and sisters everywhere; America, Africa, all over the world, years where pleasure and pain were mixed together. I knew then, and I still do, that the happiness I felt, and still feel, as we moved forward together was of a kind that very few people ever experience.

Discography

List of original album releases

Bethlehem: 1958

Jazz as Played . . .
Nina Simone and Her Friends

Colpix: 1959–1963

The Amazing . . .
Town Hall
Newport
Forbidden Fruit
Village Gate
Sings Ellington
Carnegie Hall
Folksy
With Strings

Philips: late 1963–1966

In Concert
Broadway
Put a Spell . . .
Pastel Blues
Let it all Out
Wild is the Wind
High Priestess

RCA: late 1966–1973

Sings Blues
Silk & Soul

'Nuff Said!
And Piano
Love Somebody
Black Gold
Here Comes the Sun
Emergency Ward
It is Finished

Stroud: from live 60s and 70s material

Live Europe (double)
Portrait (double)
Black is the Colour (double)
Berkeley
Sings Billie Holiday
Gospel
Town Hall Revisited
Lamentations
Don't Let Me be Misunderstood

Miscellaneous

In Concert (Oxford)
Baltimore (CTI) 1978
Very Rare Evening (PM)
Fodder in Her Wings (Carrere) 1982
Featuring . . . (Spinorama)
Live at Vine St (Polygram)
Nina's Back! (Videopix)

**If you would like to join the
International Nina Simone Fan Club,
please write to:**

Roger Nupie
Boudewijnsstraat 103
2018 Antwerpen 1
Belgium

Index